WOOD PALLET WONDERS

DIY PROJECTS FOR HOME, GARDEN, HOLIDAYS AND MORE

BECKY LAMB

Ulysses Press

This book is dedicated to my family.
You support and love me unconditionally, and inspire me to be better each day.

Published in the U.S. by:
Ulysses Press
P.O. Box 3440
Berkeley, CA 94703
www.ulyssespress.com

ISBN: 978-1-61243-755-2
Library of Congress Control Number: 2017952138

Printed in the United States by Bang Printing
10 9 8 7 6 5 4 3 2 1

Acquisitions editor: Casie Vogel
Managing editor: Claire Chun
Editor: Shayna Keyles
Proofreader: Renee Rutledge
Front cover design: Michelle Thompson
Interior design: what!design @ whatweb.com
Layout: Jake Flaherty

Distributed by Publishers Group West

CONTENTS

INTRODUCTION

Since writing my first book, *Crafting with Wood Pallets*, some things have changed in my life: My family moved into an 85-year-old schoolhouse, and I now only have one child left at home. But my love for building and using pallets has not changed. The large workshop that I gained when we moved into our new home has made building and creating easier. We also have many more home projects to work on with our old schoolhouse and larger property, and many of those are being done with pallet wood. Currently, we are working on a floating deck made from pallets, using pallet wood to create a shiplap wall, and creating a pallet laundry supply storage solution.

As a blogger at *Beyond the Picket Fence*, I get a lot of questions from readers about me and what I do. I thought I would introduce myself to you by answering some of these common questions.

How do you get your ideas? I was blessed to have a creative mother with a do-it-yourself attitude, and I believe I learned many of my creative habits from her. I do think that creativity can be taught, and I am thankful to have been raised in a home that encouraged it. I see ideas everywhere, and the smallest thing will spark my imagination. I see ideas by looking at a piece of junk in a different way, by getting out in nature to refresh my creativity, and from our household needs. For example, if I need a nightstand, I figure out how to make one from pallet wood in the style that I want.

Why do you build with pallet wood? I have always seen the value in reusing whatever I can. I do not like the idea of pallets made from good wood filling our landfills. I also enjoy the challenge of creating with pallets and having the ability to make something unique. As a family of educators (my husband is a high school principal and taught elementary school for 25 years), we have always lived on a budget, and free pallets fit that budget. I like a rustic, eclectic, industrial style, and pallet furniture works well with my décor.

Do you really make everything you share? I do indeed make all of my own projects. But I am thankful for my husband of 29 years, who helps me when I need it and who taught me how to use power tools. There are only a couple of places in the book that I mention using a table saw as an option, because I have just never been very comfortable with it. My husband will make table saw cuts for me. He and my three children (two of whom are now in their twenties) have all helped me over the years when I was in a bind—they have sanded and painted, hauled and dismantled pallets, and found treasures for me to repurpose.

What else do you enjoy doing besides building with pallets and reclaimed wood? When I am not in my workshop, I love participating in various outdoor activities in my beautiful home state of Montana. As a family, we enjoy hiking, camping, biking, floating the rivers, and paddleboarding. We also enjoy gardening in our 1,500 square-foot greenhouse (another bonus of moving into our old schoolhouse) and working on projects around our home.

What do I need to know about building with pallets? This book will provide you will all of the information you need to get started building with pallets. I want readers to know that you need to be patient with yourself, especially if you are a beginning woodworker. I make mistakes—inaccurate cuts, drilling through wood where I am not supposed to, spilling entire cans of paint, etc.—all the time. I also learn from the mistakes. When I was creating the last project for this book and made a mistake, I told my husband that I should have been taking pictures of all of the mistakes and included a bloopers chapter in the book. Also, remember that you are completing all of these projects at your own risk. Please use all safety precautions and procedures when using power tools and creating any project in the book. Follow all manufacturer instructions.

Pallets are easy to build with, but they vary greatly. I provide exact measurements for the projects, but you may need to alter things slightly to fit the size of the boards you are using. Be sure to read through all of the directions before starting a project. Change up projects when you need and want to personalize them to meet your needs. And remember to enjoy the process.

PALLETS 101: EVERYTHING YOU NEED TO KNOW

FINDING PALLETS

Once I decided I wanted to build with pallets, I needed to find some. One drive around my small town and I discovered plenty of sources of quality pallets: a flooring store, a heating and air conditioning business, a plumbing supply store, a glass shop, and the local newspaper. I always go into the business and ask if pallets are free for the taking. Most often, the business is thrilled that someone wants to take pallets off their hands. Also, pallets are often listed in the "free section" of classified ads. Once you find a couple of good sources, you will know where to look for the perfect pallet for a particular project.

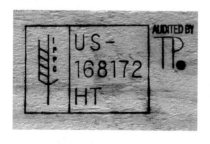

WHAT TO LOOK FOR WHEN PICKING PALLETS

After you discover where to find free pallets, you need to know what to look for, because not all pallets are created equal. Most important: Look for the IPPC (International Plant Protection Convention) label or the HT stamp on the pallet.

The IPPC identifier means that the manufacturer has followed the regulated international standard for treating pallets. The HT identifier means that the pallet wood has been heat treated, rather than chemically treated. Do not use a pallet if you do not see the IPPC label or the HT stamp. Pallets that are only for domestic shipping may not have the IPPC label, but you can only be sure they are safe if they have the label. The stamp also shows the pallet's country of origin. The country of origin is not important as long as the pallet has the IPPC label. Most of the pallets I use are from the U.S.; a few are from Canada. In addition, check the pallet for anything that looks like chemical or oil residue. Stay away from any suspect pallets—it is not worth the risk of getting something unknown on your skin or in your lungs. Many pallets have black skid marks on them from transport. These pallets are safe to use, and most often the marks can be easily sanded off.

Next, look for pallets that are solid. Check the individual boards for cracks and splits in the wood. Almost every pallet has one or two unusable boards, so choose pallets that have mostly good boards. Some of the split boards can be glued back together and used. Look at the 2" × 4" pallet runner boards (support boards)—do you need straight boards or notched ones for your project? Choose a pallet with boards in the width required for the project. Also, find pallets made from different types of wood so that you have a variety of wood types for various projects. Lighter pallets are probably made from pine or cedar. Heavier pallets are probably made from harder woods, such as oak, hickory, and even cherry. In addition, looking at the wood grain helps to identify the wood type.

TOOLS AND EQUIPMENT

I have collected a nice selection of tools over the years, but I started with the most basic equipment: hammer, saw, drill, and sander. Many of the pallet projects in this book can be built using an inexpensive jigsaw, a small cordless drill, and a palm sander. Nicer, better tools do make the work easier, and I generally find that you get what you pay for. But the best tools aren't necessary to complete these projects. Buy the best tools you can afford, and then upgrade when you are able to. Good-quality used tools are often available at garage sales, pawn shops, and online sale sites.

SAFETY. It is important to use tools safely. Read and follow all safety instructions for the tools you are using. Always wear safety goggles when using any power tools. Wear gloves, especially to protect against rough wood and slivers. A respirator mask or a dust mask is important to wear while sanding.

SAWS. A jigsaw or another type of reciprocating saw, such as a Sawzall, are the best tools for taking pallets apart. Saw blades made for cutting metal are necessary for cutting through nails. These blades are usually painted white, blue, or yellow. I recommend a corded saw as opposed to a cordless version. A cordless saw does not have enough power and needs to be recharged often.

A miter saw is the most accurate and provides the quickest way to cut pallet boards to different lengths, or to cut angles. You also could use a jigsaw, a circular saw, or a handsaw instead. For cutting angles, you can use the power miter saw or a handsaw with an inexpensive miter box. A band saw also is helpful for making some specialty cuts.

HAMMER AND MINI PRYBAR. A hammer with a good claw (the forked end used for removing nails) and a mini crowbar or prybar are needed to take apart a pallet and to remove nails.

CLAMPS. Clamps in a variety of sizes are invaluable for keeping wood pieces in place when drilling and screwing, and for holding wood together when gluing. They serve as a second pair of "hands."

ELECTRIC SANDER. An electric sander makes the job of sanding rough pallet wood much easier. Palm sanders are small, lightweight, and easy to use. There are different types of electric palm sanders. A random orbit sander has a round sanding pad that spins when sanding, while an orbital sander usually has a square sanding pad that vibrates. You can buy hook and loop sandpaper, adhesive sandpaper, or regular sandpaper that attaches to the sander one quarter of a sheet at a time. Check to see what type of sandpaper your sander uses, as all sanders are different. I use a random orbit sander because it works more quickly than an orbital sander. This sander also has a variable speed dial; most orbital sanders do not.

I most often use two different grits of sandpaper. The larger the number on the sandpaper, the finer the grit. For unfinished pallet wood I generally use 60 grit, or coarse, sandpaper because the wood is rough. I use 120 or 150 grit for finish sanding and for sanding paint.

CORDLESS DRILL AND DRILL BITS. A cordless drill is one of those tools you will wonder how you ever got along without. I started with the cheapest one and over the years traded up. You want a drill that has at least a 12-volt battery; mine has an 18-volt. I now own two drills. I keep a drill bit to drill holes on one drill and a Phillips-head screw bit on the other. I like using smaller, lightweight drills as long as they have a decent-sized battery.

In addition to a cordless drill, you also need a set of drill bits. I usually buy extra drill bits in the sizes I use the most (for example, size $^3/_{32}$") because sometimes they break off. I typically predrill all holes before adding screws so that the pallet wood does not split when screwing in the screw.

A countersink bit drills out a small circle for the screw head as it is drilling the hole for the screw so that the screw will sit flush with the wood. I typically use a countersink bit for all of the predrilled holes. In the directions when a countersink hole is necessary, I mention using a countersink bit.

BRAD NAILER OR BRAD GUN. For a few projects I use a brad nailer, or brad gun, to attach wood pieces. I do this when I don't want too many screws showing; for example, when attaching wood pieces for a tabletop. My brad nailer works with an air compressor and uses skinny "nails," or brads. There are some brad nailers that are electric and do not require an air compressor. If you don't have a brad nailer, small finish nails and a hammer can be used. Small finish nails have a little bit of a larger head than a brad and work equally well, but take more time.

SCREWS. You'll need a variety of screws for the projects in this book. I buy screws in bulk, paying by the pound, at my local hardware store. I sort the screws by size and keep them in empty nut and candy containers, and I write the screw size on the lid. I use Phillips-head screws.

TAPE MEASURE. A tape measure is essential. I have a couple: I keep one by my saw and one in my toolbox.

PAINTBRUSHES. I mostly use brushes called chip brushes or natural bristle brushes. They are inexpensive and leave a rougher finish, which I like on pallet wood. I prefer nylon bristle brushes, which leave fewer brush marks, for use with chalkboard paint.

PICTURE-HANGING HARDWARE. Many of the projects in this book require picture-hanging hardware. For an item that is heavy or might become off-balance when something is placed on it (like a coat hook), I use ½" D-rings or 2-hole D-rings on the back. D-rings come with their own screws to secure them to the project. I hang other items with 40-pound picture-hanging wire and screws (usually ¾" or 1").

TAKING APART PALLETS

Taking apart pallets does require some time and work. The job is easier with two people, but I have taken apart many pallets by myself. Please use extra caution when disassembling pallets: Always wear protective eyewear, long pants, and close-toed shoes. Be conscious of where your saw cord is while cutting so that you do not nick it or cut through it.

USING A RECIPROCATING SAW

The quickest and easiest way to cut wood off a pallet is to use a reciprocating saw, such as a Sawzall, with a blade for cutting metal. The long blade easily slips between the pallet wood pieces to cut the nails holding them together. Have someone hold the pallet for you or steady the pallet by keeping your foot on the bottom board while you cut. This method will leave nail parts in the wood, especially in the 2" × 4" pieces. A handheld jigsaw fitted with a metal blade will also take apart a pallet, although the jigsaw blade is not as long as the blade on a Sawzall type of reciprocating saw.

A tool called a pallet buster (see Resources on page 124) allows you to easily remove boards from pallet runners. It uses leverage to remove the boards with the nails. After removing the boards with the pallet buster, use a hammer to remove the nails. I like using this method because it allows you to have boards with no nails in them. It does take longer than using a Sawzall to dismantle a pallet.

A mini crowbar or prybar and a hammer provide another way to remove pallet boards. This method is more work, but I often use it when removing just one or two boards, or when I want to remove all of the nails from the boards. Hammer the mini crowbar in between the pallet boards to wedge them apart and loosen the nail heads. Use the hammer claw to pull out the nails.

To cut pallet parts from a pallet without completely removing the boards, use a handheld jigsaw or circular saw.

A reciprocating saw like a Sawzall can also be used to cut pallet wood, but the cut usually isn't as accurate or straight.

USING A JIGSAW

If a board is unusable, I put it in the burn pile for our fire pit. Some split boards can be clamped and repaired with wood glue. Be sure to get the glue into the crack or split, and then clamp tightly. Remove any excess glue with a rag or paper towel before it dries. Let the glue dry for 24 hours before unclamping and using the board.

After you take apart a couple of pallets and learn what works best, the job will become easier. I usually disassemble five or more pallets at a time, and it takes me approximately 30 to 45 minutes to take apart five pallets with a reciprocating saw like a Sawzall.

PALLET PARTS

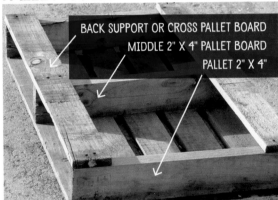
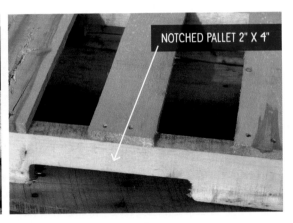

The photos above will help you identify the different parts of a pallet. I refer to the main support boards as 2" × 4" pallet runner boards. Although they are often a bit smaller than typical 2" × 4" boards, in this book, they are called 2" × 4"s for easy reference.

PALLET SIZES

Pallets come in a wide variety of sizes. I have used pallets that are as small as 12" × 24" and ones that are as large as 48" × 120". Smaller-sized pallets most often tend to be 20" × 32" or 36" × 36", while larger-sized pallets are usually 40" × 48" or 48" × 48". I list sizes of pallets I used for the projects in the book, but you will need to be flexible and adjust measurements and boards needed according to the size of the pallet you are using if you cannot find one in the same size.

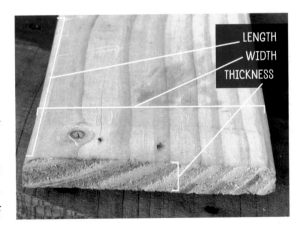

ADDING COLOR: PAINTING TECHNIQUE

I love paint. It transforms objects inexpensively, adds color, is easy to change, and is fun to play with. Over the years, I have experimented with many different painting techniques and ideas. I discovered that pallet wood is the perfect canvas for paint. My technique produces a weathered finish that appears to have been painted several times over many years. Personalize my technique to fit your needs, using the colors that you like to decorate with and enjoy.

SUPPLIES

Paint in a variety of colors ranging from light to dark. I mostly use different brands of interior latex in an eggshell finish. Latex paint, which is a water-based paint that cleans up with water, comes in five finishes: flat, eggshell, satin, semi-gloss, and gloss. Flat paint has no sheen and stains easily, while gloss paint produces the shiniest finish. I like the eggshell finish because it has a little sheen without being too glossy. Also, the glossier the paint is, the more it will "gum up" your sandpaper. I use a white semi-gloss paint for lettering signs because the stain I use to weather the wood will not stick to the semi-gloss paint and therefore, the white stays white. You can also use a gloss paint.

Another type of paint that I like to use is mineral paint made by Fusion Mineral Paint (see Resources on page 124). This paint has great coverage, dries quickly, and sticks well to many different types of surfaces.

There are a few times in the book where I use craft paint rather than latex. I use this when I need only a small amount of paint in a certain color. I prefer Waverly's Super Premium Acrylic Paint. Here are some of the supplies you'll want to have on hand:

- Paint
- Electric sander or sandpaper (For hand sanding, use 120 or 150 grit, depending on how much paint you want removed.)
- 3 or 4 paintbrushes, 1½" wide
- Stain (I often use the colors Early American or Dark Walnut.)
- Clear finish or coconut oil
- Rags (old T-shirts)
- Gloves

TECHNIQUE

1. Paint several pallet boards at once for current and future projects. Lay a variety of pallet boards on a drop cloth or a piece of cardboard. If you want more of the wood to show through the paint, do not sand the boards before painting. If you want the boards to be mostly all painted, sand the wood before painting.

2. I use three brushes, usually inexpensive chip brushes or natural hair brushes. I always keep at least one paintbrush for painting with red paint only. It is difficult to remove all of the red paint from the brush, and it will taint other colors.

3. Start by painting with the lightest colors. Here, I started with golden yellow and moss green. Do not paint every board. On the boards you paint, do not completely cover the wood with paint. This allows more colors to come through the paint layers. By the end, some boards will have three or four colors on  them, some only two. I do not clean my paintbrushes between colors. I do try to "paint off" most of the color from the brush before changing colors.

4. When the paint is mostly dry, paint the next lightest colors, such as bright green and light blue. Do not completely cover the previous colors.

5. Continue with your paint colors, applying the darker colors over the lighter ones.

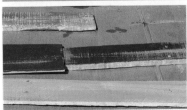

6. When the paint is fairly dry, use the lightest colors again to paint a few of the boards. This creates a handful of boards with light colors on the top layer, for variety.

7. Clean the paintbrushes with warm water and a small amount of liquid dish soap.

8. When the paint is dry, sand the boards with 120 or 150 grit sandpaper. Use the 120 grit if you want to remove more paint, 150 grit if you want the paint removal to be a little more subtle. The paint will come off easily from the rough areas of the pallet wood. Sanding will reveal the colors under the top paint color. Some exposed wood with no paint on it is desirable.

9. Next, apply stain over the painted boards, and be sure to wear gloves to protect your hands. Use a chip brush reserved for stain, and completely cover the paint. Wipe the excess stain off with a rag, and properly dispose of used rags according to the stain manufacturer's directions.

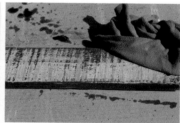

10. Wait to apply a clear finish until you use the boards in a project. The type of project will determine the finish. The type of clear finish that I use most often is an acrylic spray-on sealer made for both indoor and outdoor use. I also use a brush-on polyacrylic, which creates a thicker protective finish than the spray-on sealer. Be watchful for drips with a brush-on finish. In addition, I like coconut oil (used frequently in cooking) as a finish, especially over unpainted wood. It is all-natural, does not get rancid, and brings out the wood's natural colors. It should not be used on outdoor pieces. Coconut oil does provide a protective finish, but not as strong as the acrylic sealers do.

SPRING

Spring often takes its sweet time arriving in Montana. When we see the first robins and the first grape hyacinth peeking through the snow, we know warmer days are on the way. I enjoy planning my garden and buying and planting annuals and perennials in the spring. I love seeing the return of songbirds and spending time outdoors observing the burgeoning spring. I also like using more color in my home in the spring, especially the softer, pastel colors. These spring projects are designed to help you enjoy the best parts of spring.

BIRDHOUSE APARTMENTS

We love our feathered friends, and each year when I see the first robin, I know spring is just around the corner. Encourage birds to nest in your yard by building an adorable "apartment" for them. This birdhouse provides a safe and cozy nesting place for a trio of birds.

SUPPLIES

- Four 48" x 5¼" x ½" pallet boards
- Two 48" x 3½" x ½" pallet boards
- One 48"-long ¼" dowel

- 1¼" screws
- 1" screws
- Outdoor paint
- Paintbrush
- Clear outdoor sealer

- Stain
- Two heavy-duty D-rings

TOOLS

- Miter saw
- Palm sander
- Drill
- 1½" hole saw bit
- ¹⁹/₆₄" drill bit
- Tape measure
- Clamp

TIME: 1½ hours, plus dry time   **LEVEL:** Intermediate

1. Measure and cut four 15" x 5¼" x ½" pallet boards and four 10½" x 5¼" x ½" pallet boards from two of the 48" x 5¼" x ½" pallet boards. These will make the front and back of the birdhouse.

2. Measure and cut one 21¼" x 5¼" x ½" pallet board from the third 48" x 5¼" x ½" pallet boards. This will be the base of the bird house.

3. Measure and cut two 6½" x 5¼" x ½" pallet boards and two 11¼" x 5¼" x ½" pallet boards from the remaining 48" x 5¼" x ½" pallet boards, and eight 7½" x 3½" x ½" pallet boards from the 48" x 3½" x ½" boards. These will be the walls and roof of the birdhouse.

4. Cut three 3" pieces from the ¼" dowel. Sand all of the cut pallet board pieces.

5. Using a miter saw, cut 20-degree angles from one end of each of the 15" x 5¼" x ½" and 10½" x 5¼" x ½" boards. Save two of the triangles that you cut off.

6. Using 1¼" screws, attach the four front boards to the 21¼" x 5¼" x ½" pallet board, drilling two screws through each board. To keep the boards sturdy while screwing, prop

them up on one of the 11¼" x 5¼" x ½" wall boards.

7. Using 1" screws, secure the top two middle boards together with one of the triangles you saved in step 5.

8. Before adding the four angled boards to the other side of the base, use 1" screws to connect the two middle boards in the second set of 10½" x 5¼" x ½" angled boards with the second triangle. You need to do this *before* attaching the boards to the bottom of the birdhouse on the other side, because the drill will not fit between the sides.

9. Attach the second set of angled boards to the other side of the base of the birdhouse with 1¼" screws.

10. Place the two 6½" x 5¼" x ½" boards on the ends of the birdhouse. Use a clamp if necessary; I did not need one. Secure the boards in place with two 1¼" screws drilled through the front and back sides of the bird house.

11. Place the 11¼" x 5¼" x ½" walls inside the birdhouse, separating the shorter angled boards from the taller ones. Hold in place with a clamp.

12. Secure the middle boards using two 1¼" screws per side, drilled through the front and back sides of the birdhouse.

13. Measure and mark 4¾" up from the bottom of the birdhouse on the shorter birdhouses and 8½" up from the bottom of the taller middle birdhouse. Using the 1½" hole saw bit, drill a hole at each mark.

See the Pallet Pointers on page 18 if you want to change the size of the opening for the type of bird that you hope to have nest in the birdhouse. Hand-sand around the hole.

14. Attach the eight 7½" x 3½" x ½" boards to the angled tops to create the roof. I used only two 1¼" screws for each roof piece so that they are easy to remove when you clean out the birdhouse in the fall. You will notice there is a small space between the tallest birdhouse and the roof of the shorter birdhouses, which is not noticeable and will not affect the birds.

15. Measure and mark 2" down from each birdhouse opening.

16. Using the ¹⁹/₆₄" drill bit, drill a hole at each mark for the dowel perch.

17. Before adding the perches, paint the birdhouses as desired. I painted each one a different color.

18. When the paint is dry, dip each 3" dowel in wood glue, and place the dowels in the holes. It should be a tight fit, and you may need to "screw" the dowel pieces in.

19. To finish the birdhouse, I stained the roof and perches. Finish with a clear coat of outdoor sealant.

20. Attach two heavy-duty D-rings on the back to hang the birdhouse on a fence or the side of your house or shed. You also could secure the birdhouse to the top of a wood ladder to set in your garden area.

PALLET POINTERS
BIRDHOUSE OPENINGS

- Ash-Throated Flycatcher: 1½"
- Barn Owl: 6"
- Black-Capped Chickadee: 1⅛"
- Carolina Chickadee: 1⅛"
- Carolina Wren: 1½"
- Downy Woodpecker: 1¼"
- Eastern Bluebird: 1½"
- House Finch: 2"
- House Wren: 1¼"
- Northern Flicker: 2½"
- Prothonotary Warbler: 1⅛"
- Purple Martin: 2½"
- Tree Swallow: 1⅜"
- Tufted Titmouse: 1¼"
- Violet-Green Swallow: 1½"
- White-Breasted Nuthatch: 1¼"

PALLET PLANTERS

Planting season in Montana is short. When spring rolls around, I am always anxious to fill planters with annuals and herbs. I decorate my porch, deck, and flowerbeds with several different flower-packed planters. This easy pallet planter has a simple and clean style that can be changed up with paint and finishing. A pair of these planters looks fantastic flanking a front door.

SUPPLIES (PER PLANTER):

- Two 2" x 4" pallet runner boards
- Four 48" x 5½" x ½" pallet boards
- 1¼" screws
- Outdoor paint
- Paintbrush
- Clear outdoor sealer
- Weed fabric (optional)

TOOLS

- Saw
- Palm sander
- Drill
- Tape measure
- Clamp

TIME: 1 hour, plus dry time

LEVEL: Beginner

1. Cut four 15"-long pieces from the pallet runner 2" x 4" boards.

2. Cut eight 16" x 5½" x ½" and three 13½" x 5½" x ½" pallet boards from the 48" x 5½" x ½" pallet boards.

3. Sand all of the wood pieces. Because I wanted only the legs of the planter painted, I painted the four 2" x 4" leg pieces white before assembling the planter.

4. Place two of the 2" x 4" legs flat on your work surface and lay two of the 16" pallet boards on top of them, making sure the top board's edge is flush with the top of the legs, and the sides of the boards are flush and straight. Secure the 16" planter side boards to the legs by drilling four 1¼" screws to each 16" board. Repeat with the other two 2" x 4" legs and 16" pallet boards so that you have two sides.

5. Create the third side of the planter by joining the two planter sides you created in step 4 with two of the 16"-long pallet boards, using four 1¼" screws per board. You may want to use a clamp.

6. Secure the final two 16" boards with 1¼" screws to create the fourth side of the planter. Use a clamp to square up the sides and hold the boards in place.

7. Turn the planter upside down, with the legs pointing up in the air, and screw the 13½" boards to the bottom of the planter using four 1¼" screws per board. Screw into the pallet boards where they meet the ½" edges of the planter sides. Be sure to pre-drill to prevent the wood from splitting.

Leave spaces between the boards to allow for drainage.

8. Finish the planter with a clear coat made for the outdoors. I like to use Minwax Helmsman Spar Urethane. Be sure to clear-coat both the inside and outside of the planter.

9. I used 14" plastic pots with saucers inside the planters because it makes cleanup in the fall easier. If you choose to plant directly in the planters, lay weed fabric down in the bottom to prevent losing too much dirt through the bottom spaces.

PALLET POINTERS

CLEAR FINISHES

Be sure to choose the right clear finish for your projects. If the project is going to be used outside or exposed to a lot of moisture, use a spar urethane. Urethane is oil based, so you will need to use paint thinner to clean your brush or use an inexpensive, disposable chip brush. Urethane will yellow some over time.

Polyacrylic is a water-based finish and is suitable for most indoor projects. It comes in sheens that range from matte to glossy. A matte finish is ideal for signs that might otherwise catch a glare if finished in a glossier clear coat. It is also good if you prefer a more rustic and natural look. I most often use a semi-gloss finish because it gives a bit of sheen without too much gloss. A high-gloss finish is perfect for a more modern look.

A spray-on clear coat is quick and easy and also comes in a variety of finishes.

It does not offer as much protection as polyacrylic or urethane. It is best when you want a light finish on your project. Use it for items that do not get a lot of wear and tear.

Waxes give wood a natural look and sheen. The more you buff something coated in wax, the glossier it becomes. Wax is more time consuming and tedious to apply, but it gives a beautiful, time-worn look to wood and paint. Waxes are only appropriate for indoor use.

Coconut oil from the grocery store is a natural alternative to wax and is easy to apply. It soaks into wood quickly and will harden over time. It is perfect for projects that you want to ensure are food safe. It will need to be reapplied every once in a while. Like wax, it can be buffed with a soft cloth to create more shine.

GARDEN TOOL STOOL

I love to garden. What I don't love is kneeling to weed and plant. My desire to sit while gardening, coupled with a need to have my most used garden tools nearby, resulted in the garden tool stool. This sturdy stool is easy to carry (using the handle hole in the middle of the seat), and has a handy shelf perfect for garden gloves, trowels, and clippers.

SUPPLIES

- Three 48" x 5½" x ½" pallet boards
- Two 48" x 3½" x ½" pallet boards
- Pencil
- 1¼" screws
- Outdoor paint
- Paintbrush
- Stencils (optional)
- Clear outdoor sealer

TOOLS

- Miter saw
- Table saw, band saw, or scroll saw
- Jigsaw
- Palm sander
- Drill
- Tape measure
- Straightedge
- Clamp
- Countersink bit

TIME: 1½ hours, plus dry time   **LEVEL:** Intermediate

1. From the 48" x 5½" x ½" pallet boards, cut two 20" x 5½" x ½" boards, four 11" x 5½" x ½" boards, and two 15" x 5½" x ½" pallet boards.

2. From the two 48" x 3½" x ½" pallet boards, cut two 15" x 3½" x ½" boards and two 11" x 3½" x ½" boards.

3. Measure and mark halfway across the width of the two 11" x 3½" x ½" boards. Use the straightedge to draw a line lengthwise down the center of the boards. Using a table saw, a band saw, or a scroll saw, cut the boards in half lengthwise to make four braces for the stool.

4. Sand all of the wood pieces.

5. On the four 11" x 5½" pieces, measure and mark 2½" in on the 5½" side.

6. Using a miter saw, cut a 30-degree angle from the 2½" mark on each of the four 11" x 5½" pieces to remove the corner.

7. Join two of the 11" x 5½" pieces together with two of the braces you cut in step 3 to create a stool leg, drilling four 1¼" screws into each brace. Place the top brace flush with the top of the 11" pieces, and place the bottom brace right above the upside-down V created by the corners cut off in step 6. Repeat to create a second leg.

8. Set the two 15" x 5½" x ½" pallet boards on top of the bottom brace to form the stool shelf. Use four 1¼" screws per board to secure the shelf to the bottom leg braces.

You can use a clamp, if needed, to help hold the shelf in place.

9. Add the sides of the stool shelf by drilling the 15" x 3½" x ½" boards in place with two 1¼" screws per board, screwing through the outside edges of the stool legs.

10. Set the two 20" x 5½" x ½" pallet boards together for the stool top. Measure and mark 8 inches in from both of the short edges of the boards toward the middle.

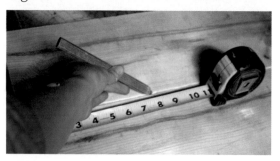

11. Between the two marks, draw a 4"-long oval for a hole for the handle, half an oval on each 20" board. I simply freehanded the oval, but you could use a template printed from the computer.

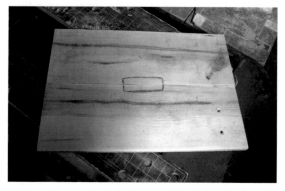

12. Use a jigsaw or scroll saw to cut the oval out. Hand sand the handle hole cut-out.

13. At this point, finish your stool as desired. I used a fun, melon-colored paint that makes the stool easy to see among the green plants.

14. Attach the 20" stool top pieces by evenly placing them on the stool base and screwing through the top, using 1¼" screws. Be sure to predrill and countersink the screws. Touch up the screws with paint.

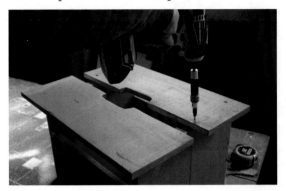

15. Using Waverly stencils, I stenciled the word GROW on the stool top. I always like to chalk the design first, to make sure my placement is even. Finish the stool with a spray-on clear urethane finish.

PALLET POINTERS

This stool not only works great in the garden, but is also the perfect stool for a child—store books and stuffed animals in the shelf. Use it in the garage and store your oil-changing tools in the bottom, or put it to work in a craft room to reach tall shelves and to keep all of your favorite crafting supplies handy.

POTTING SOIL BIN

If you love digging in the dirt and planting flowers in the spring, you no doubt have bags of potting soil. The problem is, the plastic bags of soil always seem to spill and are unsightly. A big bin with a hinged lid is the answer. It stores your potting soil perfectly and looks fantastic in your potting shed or outdoor space.

SUPPLIES

- Ten 48" x 5½" x ¾" pallet boards
- Five 48" x 3½" x ¾" pallet boards
- One 2" x 4" pallet runner board
- 1¼" screws
- 1⅝" screws
- Eight 2" screws
- Two 1½" utility hinges
- Outdoor paint
- Paintbrush
- Clear outdoor sealer

TOOLS

- Saw
- Palm sander
- Drill
- Tape measure
- Clamps (2 large, one small)
- Countersink bit
- Straightedge

TIME: 2 hours, plus dry time   **LEVEL:** Intermediate

1. Cut ten 26"-long pieces from the 48" x 5½" x ¾" pallet boards for the side of the bin. From the leftover 5½" x ¾" pallet board pieces, cut two 17¾"-long pieces and two 14¾"-long pieces.

2. For the trim, cut five 17¾"-long pieces and four 12½"-long pieces from the 48" x 3½" x ¾" pallet boards. From the leftover pallet board pieces, cut two 10"-long pieces.

3. Cut two 11"-long boards from the 2" x 4" runner board.

4. Lightly sand all of the pallet boards.

5. Create one of the narrower sides of the bin by placing two of the 26" x 5½" x ¾" boards perpendicular to two of the 12½" x 3½" x ¾" outside trim boards, with one 12½"-long board at either end of the 26"-inch long boards. Leave an equal ¾" overhang on either side.

6. Screw the boards together using 1¼" screws, drilling two screws into each 5½" board.

7. Repeat steps 5 and 6 to make the second narrow side of the bin.

8. Turn over the sides you created in steps 5 to 7 and secure one 11" x 2" x 4" board flush against one of the short edges of each, using 4 of the 2" screws per bin side. This will form a brace to secure the bottom of the bin to.

9. Repeat steps 5 and 6 to create the wider front and back sides of the bin, this time using three 26" x 5½" x ¾" boards and two 17¾" x 3½" x ¾" trim boards per side. Remember to leave a ¾" overhang on each side. Make two sides this way.

10. Connect the narrow sides by placing the two 14¾" x 5½" x ¾" boards on top of the 2" x 4" braces. Secure the 14¾" boards to the braces with 1¼" screws, two per board.

11. Rest one of the wider bin sides on top of the partially connected bin, lining up the trim boards at the corners. Use two large clamps to square up the bin and to hold the sides in place.

12. Secure the sides together at the corners, using two 1⅝" screws per corner. Be sure to countersink the screws.

On two of the corners, I needed to use a smaller clamp on the trim boards to ensure they were squarely aligned.

13. To further secure the bin sides together, add four 1⅝" screws to the front of each wider bin side at points A, B, C, and D, with two screws 8" from the top edge and two screws 8" from the bottom of the bin.

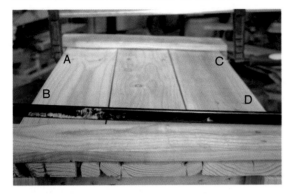

14. Repeat steps 11 through 13 with the fourth side.

15. To create the lid, place the one leftover 17¾" x 3½" x ¾" trim board between the two 17¾" x 5½" x ¾" boards and connect them with the two 10" x 3½" x ¾" pallet boards, using two 1¼" screws per 17¾" board. Place the joiner boards 2½" from the lid sides and about 2" from the top and bottom of the lid.

16. Paint as desired. I chose a nice, bright green, and left the trim boards natural. I lightly sanded the paint after it dried for a weathered look.

17. When the paint is dry, place the lid on top of the bin, lining up the edge of the lid with the back side of the bin. This will provide a lip on the front of the bin, which will allow you to easily open the lid.

18. Secure the hinges by screwing them into the edge of the lid and the edge of the top trim piece on the back of the bin. I prefer to use 1¼" screws, rather than the screws that come with the hinge.

19. Finish the potting soil bin with a clear coat. I clear-coated the inside of the lid, but not the inside of the bin. Depending on how you are going to use the bin, you might want to clear coat the inside, as well.

HANGING FLOWER POCKET

In Montana, life can be white all winter long. So when spring rolls around, I crave color. This hanging wall pocket is the perfect way to greet guests with a pop of cheery color and a hint of the spring flowers to come. You can fill this wood pocket with fresh flowers, if your climate allows, or use good-looking silk flowers. This versatile wood pocket can stand on its own so can be used on a windowsill or shelf.

SUPPLIES

- Three 48" x 3½" x ½" pallet boards
- One 2" x 4" pallet runner board
- 2" screws
- Pencil

- Wood glue
- 1½" brad nails or finishing nails
- Outdoor paint
- Paintbrush

- Outdoor stain
- Dry cloth
- Clear outdoor sealer
- 24" piece of 14 gauge wire

TOOLS

- Miter saw
- Palm sander
- Drill

- Brad nailing gun or hammer
- Needle nose pliers
- Tape measure

- Straightedge
- 10-pound weight

TIME: 1 hour, plus dry time   **LEVEL:** Beginner

1. Cut eight 14"-long pieces and two 17¾"-long pieces from the 48" x 3½" x ½" pallet boards.

2. Cut two 12½"-long pieces and one 7"-long piece from the 2" x 4" pallet runner board.

3. Using a miter saw, cut a 15-degree angle on one end of each of the 12½" x 2" x 4" boards.

4. Lightly sand all of the pallet boards.

5. Create the slanted, V-shaped frame of the wall pocket by screwing the 7"-long 2" x 4" to the angled cuts on the 12½" 2" x 4" boards. Use two 2" screws per side, drilling them through the bottom of the 7"-long 2" x 4".

6. Lay four of the 14" x 3½" x ½" boards next to each other and place the V-shaped frame on top. Use a pencil to trace the outline of the frame.

7. Cut the boards on the lines drawn. You will be cutting at an approximately 15-degree angle with a miter saw. Be sure to place your saw blade on the outside of the pencil line. The bottom board will have a different angle, approximately 5 degrees.

8. Repeat steps 6 and 7 with the second set of 14" x 3½" x ½" boards.

9. Once the 14" x 3½" x ½" boards have been cut to the proper sizes, lay them in the proper order, put wood glue on the edges, and place the V-shaped frame on top. Flip the glued frame over and repeat on the other side.

10. After both sides have been glued, use a weight on top to hold the boards in place. You can use a scrap board to better distribute the pressure from the weight.

11. When the glue is dry, secure the boards to the frame with either a brad nailer or finishing nails, using four nails per 3½" x ½" board, two per side.

12. Sand the edges of the pocket to round them a bit.

13. Paint as desired. I used softer colors for spring. When the paint is dry, sand again and then stain over the paint for a weathered look. I used the Provincial stain from Minwax.

14. Wipe off the excess stain with a dry cloth. Then finish with a clear coat.

15. Use a ⅛" drill bit to drill two holes in the back top edge, approximately 2½" from each of the sides and an inch down from the top edge.

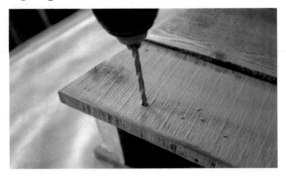

16. Place the wire through the holes from the outside.

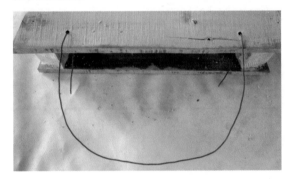

17. Use the needle-nose pliers to curl the ends of the wire to secure it.

VARIATIONS

If you want to use fresh flowers in the pocket, be sure to coat the inside with a waterproof sealer. You can also just place a couple glass bud vases inside of the pocket, flatten a plastic pot to fit in the pocket, or line it with a coconut liner. If you use silk flowers and they need a little boost to be taller, put some plastic grocery bags in the bottom.

Paint the pocket different colors to use during different seasons. You can even paint the sides of the frame white and then paint the front side of the pocket one color and the back side of the pocket a different color so you can flip the pocket to the other side for a new look.

GARDEN BENCH

When spring finally arrives, I love being outdoors. It doesn't get much better than sitting outside while enjoying the blooming lilacs and flowers and a cool drink. This small garden bench is the perfect spot to do just that. It is comfortable, and a great place to take a much-needed rest from gardening, or to just sit and enjoy the backyard.

SUPPLIES

- Five 2" x 4" pallet runner boards
- Four 48" x 5½" x ¾" pallet boards
- Three 48" x 3½" x ¾" pallet boards
- Pencil
- 1⅝" screws
- Four 2" screws
- Outdoor paint
- Paintbrush
- Clear outdoor sealer

TOOLS

- Jigsaw or band saw
- Palm sander
- Drill
- Tape measure
- Clamp
- Countersink bit
- Straightedge

TIME: 2 hours, plus dry time   **LEVEL:** intermediate

1. Cut two 34"-, two 16"-, and two 21"-long pieces from the pallet runner 2" x 4" boards.

2. Cut two 36"- and six 14"-long pieces from the 5½" x ¾" pallet boards.

3. Cut two 36"- and two 16¾"- long pieces from the 3½" x ¾" pallet boards.

4. Sand all of the wood pieces.

5. On the 34" x 2" x 4" runner boards, mark 11" down from the top of each board.

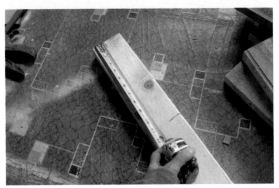

6. Mark 2" from one side on the 34" x 2" x 4" boards.

7. Using a straightedge, draw a diagonal line from the 2" mark to the edge of the board at the 11" mark.

8. Using either a handheld jigsaw or a band saw (I used a band saw), cut on the diagonal line that you drew. This is going to create a slight angle to the upper back of the bench so that it is more comfortable.

9. Mark 16" up on the two 21" x 2" x 4" boards and on the 34" x 2" x 4" boards. For the two 34"-long boards, mark on the opposite ends of the angle cuts made in step 8.

10. Using 1⅝" screws, join the 21" x 2" x 4" boards together with the 36" x 3½" x ¾" board. Align the top of the 36" board with the 16" marks that you made. Use 4 screws total, drilling two in each side.

11. Repeat step 10 to connect the two 34" x 2" x 4" boards, attaching the brace to the same side that the angle is cut on. You've now created both sets of bench legs.

12. Stand your two sets of legs up and join them together with the 14" x 5½" x ¾" boards, which will form the seat. Drill the tops of the 14" boards into the 36" x 3½" x ¾" braces with 1⅝" screws, 4 per board.

13. Secure the two end seat boards first and then add the middle boards, placing them with an even space between the boards, if needed.

14. Set the bench on its back and use 1⅝" screws, 4 per board, to attach the two 36"

x 5½" x ¾" boards to the angle you cut in step 8.

There will be about ½" space between the boards.

15. Measure and mark up 6" on the outside of the four legs.

16. Using 1⅝" screws, attach the 16¾" x 3½" x ¾" boards to brace the legs, aligning the top edge of the boards with the 6" mark. Use four screws per board. Use a clamp, if necessary, to square up the brace with the legs.

17. To form the armrest, attach the 16" x 2" x 4" boards to the top of the front legs using two 2" screws in each board.

18. Flip the bench over, and drilling at an angle, secure the back of the armrest to the back of the bench using 1⅝" screws. Be sure

to countersink your screws so they are not visible.

19. Paint the bench as desired. I used a white paint intended for outdoor use and finished the bench with a clear, outdoor sealer. The white looks fantastic and really stands out in a green garden.

PALLET POINTERS
VARIATIONS

You can make this bench longer if desired. Most pallet boards come in 48" lengths. If you add two more 14" x 5½" x ¾" seat boards, your finished bench will be approximately 47" long. You will simply need to cut 47" boards for the seat braces and for the bench back; all of the other cuts should be the same. This bench is versatile and looks fantastic in an entryway or on a porch.

SUMMER

I don't know too many people who do not love summer. We spend as much time as possible outdoors during the summer months: barbecuing with friends, playing outdoor games, hiking, camping, and fishing. The projects in this section are all about enjoying our outdoor spaces. Invite friends and family over for a backyard barbecue on the pallet Picnic Table, play a fun outdoor game, and savor the long days of summer.

PATRIOTIC STARBURST

Summertime decorating at my house takes on a casual attitude, including just a few red, white, and blue touches to my regular décor. This patriotic starburst is a fun, unique version of a "flag" and looks great above a fireplace mantel, on a porch or outdoor shed, or hanging on the gable of your home.

SUPPLIES

- Four 48" x 3½" x ½" pallet boards
- One scrap piece from a 5½" x ¾" pallet board, at least 5½" long
- 1⅝" screws
- 1" screws
- Red, white, and blue paints
- Paintbrush
- Small craft detail paintbrush
- Heavy-duty D-ring
- White chalk
- Clear sealer
- Damp cloth

TOOLS

- Miter saw, jigsaw, or band saw
- Palm sander
- Drill
- Tape measure
- Countersink bit
- Straightedge
- Star stencil (optional)
- Cloth

TIME: 1 hour, plus dry time

LEVEL: Beginner

1. Cut twelve 15"-long pieces from the 48" x 3½" x ½" pallet boards.

2. Cut the scrap 5½" pallet board into a square measuring 5½" x 5½" x ¾".

3. Lightly sand all of the pallet boards. Then find and mark the center on one end of each of the 14" x 3½" x ¾" boards.

4. Using a miter saw, a jigsaw, or a band saw, cut a 45-degree picket on one end of each 14" board, using the center mark made

in Step 3 as a guide. The pickets do not need to be perfectly even.

5. Paint four of the pickets red, four white, and four blue. I did not paint the sides or the backs.

6. Use a straightedge to find and mark the center of the 5½" x 5½" x ¾" board.

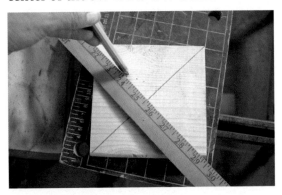

7. When the paint is dry on the pickets, attach the red boards to the 5½" square. Align the pickets and use one 1"-screw per picket. Be sure to countersink the screws.

8. Place a white picket so it makes a 30-degree angle with a red picket, matching up the tip of the picket with the middle of the red starburst. Secure with a 1⅝" screw. Once one picket is in place, the others will match up in the center. Secure each picket with a 1⅝" screw.

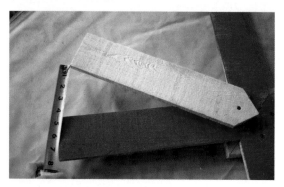

9. Place the blue pickets on top of the white starburst, spacing them evenly between the white and red pickets. Secure the boards using one 1⅝" screw per picket.

10. Screw a heavy-duty D-ring on the top middle edge on the back of the square, making sure a red picket is straight above it.

11. Using a piece of white chalk, draw stars on the blue pickets. Consider drawing a few going off the edge.

12. With a small craft paintbrush and white paint, paint the stars. You could use a star stencil if you want a more perfect star.

13. When the paint is dry, lightly sand the patriotic starburst, if desired. Wipe away any excess chalk with a damp cloth. Finish with a clear coat appropriate for where you will be using the starburst.

PALLET POINTERS
VARIATIONS

This would make a great, unique decoration for other seasons as well: paint it red, green, and white for Christmas or orange, yellow, and brown for fall. You can paint it all white for a winter snowflake, or red with white hearts for Valentine's Day. Make three starbursts in three different sizes, and use them as a grouping above a bed or on a family room wall.

FISHING POLE HOLDER

Fishing and summer in Montana go hand in hand. We are lucky enough to have great lakes, rivers, and streams that we can drop a fishing line into during long summer days. Having a place to safely store poles in between fishing trips is important. This quick project provides a functional and good-looking place to hold those rods until the next fishing outing.

SUPPLIES

- One small 32" x 20½" pallet
- One 2" x 4" pallet runner board
- Two 48" x 3½" x ¾" pallet boards
- One 5½" x ¾" pallet board, at least 22" long
- 1⅝" screws
- 2" screws
- ¾" screws
- Pencil
- Paint
- Paintbrush
- White chalk
- Stencils
- Stencil paintbrush
- Small craft detail paintbrush
- Clear sealer
- Two 4" mending or joiner plates

TOOLS

- Miter saw
- Jigsaw
- Palm sander
- Drill
- ½" drill bit
- Tape measure
- Straightedge

1. Remove the back boards from the pallet, using your preferred method of removal.

2. Cut two 10" x 2" x 4" pieces from the pallet runner board.

3. Cut two 20½"-long boards and one 23"-long board from the 48" x 3½" x ¾" boards.

4. Cut one 20½" x 5½" x ¾" board from the 5½" x ¾" board.

5. Lightly sand all of the pallet boards.

6. On one end of each of the 10" x 2" x 4" pallet boards, find and mark the center of the board.

7. Using a miter saw, cut one corner off of the end of each of the 2" x 4" boards at a 45-degree angle, starting at the mark made in step 6. This will simply give the back of the brace a more finished look; it is not structural, and this step can be skipped if desired.

8. Make the bottom base frame by securing the 23" x 3½" x ¾" board to the straight ends of the 2" x 4" boards, using two 1⅝" screws per side.

9. Fit the two 20½" x 3½" x ¾" boards into the base frame, placing them flat between the 2" x 4" side support boards. One should touch the front 23" x 3½" x ¾" board and the other should be snug against the first. These will form the bottom of the fishing pole holder base.

Secure the bottom 20½" x 3½" x ¾" boards to the base frame, drilling the screws through the side supports into the bottom boards. Use two 2" screws per board on each side.

10. Place the 32" x 20½"" pallet next to the outer 20½" x 3½" x ¾" board, with the pallet boards running perpendicular to the base. Place the pallet's bottom 2" x 4" board on top of the 20½" 3½" x ¾" base board, then secure the pallet using two 2" screws per side, screwing through the side supports into the bottom 2" x 4".

11. To further secure the pallet to the base, screw one 2" screw per side into the vertical 3½" x ¾" pallet board, screwing through the side supports into the vertical board.

12. On the 2" x 4" on top of the pallet, make a dot in the center of each vertical pallet board, 2" from the front of the 2" x 4" board, for a total of five dots.

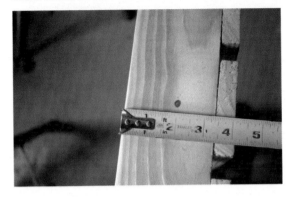

13. Using a ½" drill bit, drill a hole at each mark made in the previous step. This will give you five holes.

14. Repeat steps 13 and 14 on the middle 2" x 4" pallet board, this time making the marks 1½" back from the front. This will allow the fishing poles to tilt back into the slots.

15. Using a straightedge, draw two lines on either side of each hole in the top and middle 2" x 4"s.

16. Cut along the lines to make slots, using a handheld jigsaw. Hand sand around the fishing pole slots as necessary.

17. Paint the fishing pole holder as desired. I chose a nice blue, reminiscent of the water. I used a smaller brush to get the paint into the fishing pole holder slots. Note that pallets are not perfect, and a few boards may need to be glued. The middle 2" x 4" board on the pallet had a crack, so I glued and clamped it before painting.

18. Finish the top 20½" x 5½" x ¾" board as desired. I chose to stencil the word FISHIN'. Draw a chalk line with a straightedge to keep your stencils straight. Remember to remove excess paint from your stencil brush before stenciling by daubing the paint onto a scrap board or piece of cardboard. I like to use a small paintbrush to paint in the small spaces where the stencils connect so that it looks like hand-lettering rather than a stencil, like on the letter F.

19. I then hand lettered "Wishin' I Was" on the end in front of the FISHIN' sign (after writing it in chalk), using a small detail brush. When the paint was dry on the sign, I used a light Golden Pecan stain to darken the wood just a bit.

20. Attach the top sign to the pallet using the mending plates and ¾" screws.

21. Finish with a clear coat. I chose a spray-on clear coat.

PICNIC TABLE

Being able to enjoy meals outside in the summer is one of my favorite things about the season. This picnic table provides a great place to savor a favorite meal or a cup of coffee in the cool mornings. It is a 4'-long table; smaller than some, but perfect for four people. The sleek design, which is a little different from most picnic tables, makes it easy to get in and out of the seats. It is sturdy and sits very well in the grass, on a deck, or on a patio.

SUPPLIES

- Eight 42" x 3½" x ¾" pallet boards
- Five 2" x 4" pallet runner boards, two at least 60" long, three 48" long
- Twelve 48" x 5½" x ¾" pallet boards
- 2" screws
- 1⅝" screws
- 1¼" screws
- Small clamps
- Outdoor paint
- Scrap piece of cardboard
- Paintbrush
- Clear outdoor sealer

TOOLS

- Saw
- Palm sander
- Drill
- Tape measure

TIME: 3 hours, plus dry time   **LEVEL:** Intermediate

1. Cut eight 29" x 3½" x ¾" boards and two 11" x 3½" x ¾" boards from the 42" x 3½" x ¾" pallet boards.

2. Cut two 24" x 2" x 4" boards, four 11" x 2" x 4" boards, and two 14" x 2" x 4" boards from the pallet runner boards.

3. Cut eight 16½" x 5½" x ¾" boards from four of the 48" x 5½" x ¾" pallet boards.

4. You will be using eight of the 48" x 5½" x ¾" boards as is for the table top and bench seats. Choose eight boards that are sturdy and have good ends.

5. Sand all of the wood pieces.

6. The eight 29" x 3½" x ¾" boards will be the table legs. On each of these boards, measure and mark 13" down from the top.

7. Start creating the picnic table support brace. Place two of the 29" x 3½" x ¾" boards perpendicularly on top of one of the 14" x 2" x 4" boards to make an H, aligning the top edge of the 2" x 4" with the marks made in the previous step.

8. Secure the boards by drilling two 2" screws into each board, with the screws placed at a diagonal.

9. Center the top of the H along one of the 24" x 2" x 4" boards, keeping the edges of the H flush with the edge of the board and leaving 5" on both sides of the H.

10. Secure the legs to the 24" x 2" x 4" board using two 2" screws per leg, with the screws placed at a diagonal.

11. Place the 60" x 2" x 4" pallet runner board underneath the bottom end of the H, keeping the edges of the H flush with the edge of the runner board, and leaving 23" on both sides of the H. Secure the H using two

2" screws per leg, with the screws placed at a diagonal.

12. Turn the whole picnic table brace over and add two more 29" x 3½" x ¾" table legs directly over the first two, sandwiching the 2" x 4" boards in between. Use the 2" screws to secure the 29" boards on all three 2" x 4" boards, using two screws per intersection.

13. To make a picnic table seat brace, place the 16½" x 5½" x ¾" board in the center of one 11" x 2" x 4" board, so the boards are perpendicular. Secure the boards using two

2" screws per board, with the screws placed at a diagonal.

14. On the 60" side of the table brace, measure and mark 15" from one of the table legs.

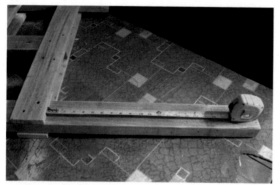

15. Place the inside edge of the seat brace at the 15" mark and secure with two 2" screws placed at a diagonal.

16. Repeat steps 13 through 15 to create and attach a second seat brace on the other end of the picnic table brace.

17. Flip the table brace over. Place one 16½" x 5½" x ¾" board directly over each of the existing 16½" x 5½" x ¾" boards, sandwiching the 11" x 2" x 4" boards in between. Secure with two 2" screws per board, with the screws placed at a diagonal.

18. Repeat steps 7 through 17 to make the second picnic table brace with seat braces.

19. Set the table braces parallel to each other and start to join them together with the eight 48" x 5½" x ¾" boards to make the table top and seats. Attach the outer table top boards and the outer seat boards before adding the inside boards to help square up the table. Align these outer boards with the outer edges of the table top braces and seat braces.

20. Secure the boards to the 2" x 4" braces, using 1⅝" screws, screwed through the 48" x 5½" x ¾" boards.

21. Secure the remaining boards, leaving an even space between the boards.

22. Using small clamps, place the 11" x 3½" x ¾" boards under the seat boards at the middle point (I used the pallet board holes from the pallet nails as my guide to find the middle of the seat boards). Secure with four

1¼" screws, screwing through the top of the seat boards.

23. Paint as desired with an outdoor latex paint. I chose white to match my house color. I dry-brushed the white color on for a weathered look. To dry brush, use a chip brush and dip just the ends of the paint-brush into your paint. Brush off a little excess paint on a piece of cardboard before painting your piece. Use a light hand when dry-brushing. I tipped the table on its side to paint the inside part first.

24. When the paint is dry, finish and pro-tect the table with a good outdoor sealer. I used spar urethane, which will yellow a bit, but it is very durable. I also used the sealer along the bottom edges of the 60" x 2" x 4" table brace to protect the wood in the moist grass.

"KUBB" LAWN GAME WITH CARRIER

My family can be fairly competitive, including when we play lawn games. And while we love a good game of cornhole, we recently discovered the ancient Viking game of Kubb (pronounced *koob*). It can be played with just two people, or with two teams with up to six people per team. The rules for Kubb are included on page 59. You can also find several videos online showing how the game is played.

SUPPLIES

- Four 48"-long 2" x 4" pallet runner boards
- One 1"-diameter wood closet rod, at least 6'6" long
- Wood glue
- Pencil
- Paint
- Paintbrush
- Painter's tape
- Stain
- Clear sealer
- Two 48" x 5½" x ¾" pallet boards
- 1⅝" screws
- Two 4-inch handles
- ¾" screws

TOOLS

- Jigsaw, band saw, or scroll saw
- Palm sander
- Drill
- Tape measure
- Clamps

TIME: 3 hours, plus dry time   **LEVEL:** Beginner

GAME PIECES

1. Glue together two sets of 48" x 2" x 4" pallet boards, making two sets of glued boards. Apply a generous amount of wood glue.

2. Secure the boards with clamps and let them dry for several hours.

3. When the glue is thoroughly dried, cut ten 6" blocks from the glued boards to make the Kubbs, or "skulls."

Then cut one 13"-long piece from the glued 2" x 4"s to make the king.

4. Cut six 12" pieces from the 1" closet rod to make the throwing "bones."

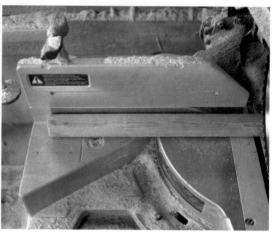

5. Find the center on one end of the king piece and free-hand draw a "crown," or a zigzag pattern. Cut out using a jigsaw, band saw, or scroll saw. This step is optional. You could paint a crown on the king piece, instead, or leave it as is.

6. Sand all of the pieces well, including the edges.

7. Paint as desired. I chose to tape off a line at the top of each game piece and then paint the pieces white with an exterior latex paint. I used a piece of tape as a guide to line up my painter's tape for the stripe.

Press the tape well to seal the edges. When the paint is dry, peel off the tape and stain the wood using a dark walnut gel stain. On the throwing sticks or bones, I did the opposite, and painted a stripe and stained the rest.

The stain over the paint will age and darken the white paint. If this is not the look you want, you can stain first and then paint over the stain once the stain is completely dry, after at least 24 hours.

8. Seal with a clear spray-on sealer when the paint is dry.

GAME CARRIER

1. Cut four 15" x 5½" x ¾" boards and two 12½" x 5½" x ¾" boards from the 48" x 5½" x ¾" pallet boards. Sand the boards.

2. Join one 15" piece to another at a 90-degree angle by drilling two 1⅝" screws from the bottom of the side of one piece into the edge of the other.

3. Repeat with the other two 15" boards. You will have two L-shaped pieces.

4. Join the two L-shaped crate sides together with one of the 12½" x 5½" x ¾" boards. Use a clamp, if necessary, to hold the end board in place and to square up the carrier. Secure the board with four 1⅝" screws, two per side.

5. Repeat step 4 on the other end of the crate.

6. Secure the 12½" sides of the crate to the bottom of the crate, using two 1⅝" screws per side.

7. Paint as desired. I chose to paint the crate to match the throwing bones by painting a stripe first and then staining it afterward.

8. When the crate is dry, center the handles on the ends, approximately 1½" down from the top edge. Secure the handles with ¾" screws.

9. Seal with a clear spray-on sealer.

KUBB GAME RULES

Goal

Be the first team to knock down all your Kubbs (skulls) and then the king. Knocking down the king without knocking down all of the skulls first is like sinking the eight ball out of turn, and results in an automatic loss.

Setup

Mark off a 16' x 26' field, called the pitch, by placing rocks in the corners. Or, you can use "gentlemen's rules" to visually determine the pitch and the out-of-bound areas. Stand the king in the center of the playing field and evenly spread five skulls along each baseline, or back rows. Each team throws one bone, or throwing stick, toward the king. The bone that lands closest to the king determines who goes first.

Game Play

1. Team 1 throws six bones at the skulls on the opposite baseline. Bones must be thrown underhand, thumb up, and must travel end over end, not helicopter style.

2. When Team 1 is finished, Team 2 stands at their baseline and throws any toppled skulls back into the other half of the field. These are now field, or pitch, skulls. Team 2 has two chances to throw each skull into the pitch. If the skull is thrown out of bounds twice in a row, the skull is placed a bone's length from the king.

3. Once all the toppled skulls have been thrown, Team 1 stands them up. If a skull was thrown into the field and it hit another skull, the skulls are stacked on top of each other, which is an advantage to the team throwing. There is no limit to how many skulls can be stacked.

4. Team 2 then must knock down all the pitch skulls before throwing at the baseline skulls. Any baseline skulls that are knocked down before the pitch skulls do not count and are stood back up. If all of the pitch skulls are knocked down and there are still bones left to throw, the remaining bones are then thrown at the baseline skulls.

5. When Team 2 is done throwing, Team 1 picks up any knocked-down skulls (both on the field and baseline) and throws them back into the opposite half of the pitch for Team 1 to stand up.

6. If Team 2 left any skulls standing, Team 1 may throw their bones from the skull closest to the king. This is a great advantage and the game may end quickly from here.

7. Play continues on this way until one team knocks over all their field and baseline skulls. That team may then attempt to knock down the king from the baseline. Once the king is knocked down, the game is over.

BARBECUE STATION

Backyard barbecues are a favorite summer tradition. We love gathering together with friends and family for great food and cold drinks to savor the long days of summer. A barbecue station that holds all of the necessary grilling supplies and has a place for cold beverages is the perfect addition to any deck or patio and makes summer entertaining convenient and easy. This station has a place for barbecue utensils, condiments, and a towel, as well as a shelf to store the barbecue cover. There is space under the shelves for a cooler to hold extra drinks and a trash can. This piece also can double as a fantastic potting bench.

SUPPLIES

- One 42" x 42" pallet—be selective when choosing a pallet for this project. Look for a pallet that has sturdy boards that are all in good shape.

- Five 2" x 4" pallet runner boards, one 42" long, four at least 36" long

- Pencil
- 1⅝" screws
- 2½" screws

- 1¼" screws
- Outdoor paint
- Paintbrush
- Wall mount bottle opener
- Small coat hook
- Two 1¼" cup hooks
- 30-quart plastic storage container
- Clear outdoor sealer

TOOLS

- Jigsaw or circular saw
- Band saw (optional)
- Palm sander
- Drill
- Tape measure
- Clamps
- Pry bar
- Straightedge

TIME: 2 hours, plus dry time   **LEVEL:** Intermediate

1. Remove the back or bottom boards from the pallet, using your preferred method of removal. Save the boards.

2. Draw a straight line on the top boards, along one outside edge of the middle runner board.

3. Using a jigsaw or circular saw, cut along the line drawn in step 2 to make the top and bottom shelves.

4. The top shelf is the half that has both 2" x 4" runner boards still attached to it. Using a pry bar or your preferred method, remove the second and third boards from the top shelf to create a place for the storage container ice bucket. You can save the boards you removed for another project.

5. The other half of the pallet that has only one 2" x 4" runner board on it needs to be cut down to make a narrower shelf to fit between the barbecue station legs. Measure and mark 16" from the outside edge of the 2" x 4", using a straightedge to draw a cutting line. Then cut along that line using a circular saw or jigsaw.

6. Attach one of the 42" x 2" x 4" runner boards along the edge of the bottom shelf boards, drilling two 1⅝" screws through each board.

7. Cut all the remaining 2" x 4" runner boards to 35" long for the legs. Be sure to trim a bit from each end of the 2" x 4"s before cutting the final 35" length so that both ends are level.

8. Sand all of the wood pieces.

9. Attach the legs to the corners on the underside of the top shelf, using clamps to hold the legs in place.

Secure the legs using four 2½" screws per leg, screwed in through the shelf's 2" x 4" runner boards.

10. Measure and mark 9" down from the top of each leg.

11. Place the bottom shelf piece between the legs, lining up the top of the shelf boards with the 9" marks on the legs. Use clamps to hold it in place.

12. Secure the bottom shelf to the legs using four 2½" screws per leg, screwed through the legs into the shelf's 2" x 4" runner boards.

13. Cut the boards that were removed in step 1 to be the same length of the top shelf boards (mine are 22½", but measure your top boards to be accurate.). Rip these boards in half vertically using a band saw or jigsaw. I used a band saw, which means the boards were not perfectly straight, but it is my preferred method. I then sanded the boards to get rid of any uneven boards.

14. Fill in the gaps on the top shelf (*not* the space for the storage container ice bucket) with the boards that were cut and ripped down in the previous step, securing them with 1⅝" screws, one screw for each end of the board. There will still be a small gap between the shelf boards, which is preferable, as it will allow rainwater to drain off the shelf.

15. Paint as desired. I used bright, tropical, sunny colors on the shelf boards only. When the paint was dry, I lightly sanded it and then stained the entire piece with Minwax Special Walnut.

16. Add a bottle opener to the leg nearest the storage container ice bucket, and attach a coat hook on the leg on the opposite end, using 1¼" screws.

17. On the end of the top shelf by the coat hook, screw two cup hooks into the edge of the shelf board to hang barbecue utensils, and set the storage container in the hole on the top shelf for ice.

18. Finish with a clear coat intended for outdoor use. I chose a spray-on clear coat.

TREE SWING

When we moved into an old school-house a few years ago, we knew one of the branches on the 85-year-old trees "needed" a tree swing. As a child, I could spend hours swinging—nothing feels more carefree than swinging under the cool shade of a big tree. This project is easy and probably the quickest one in the book, but it will last for years and be enjoyed by generations to come.

SUPPLIES

- Two sturdy 5½" x ¾" pallet boards
- One 3½" x ¾" pallet board
- 1¼" screws
- Pencil
- Four 3" x ⅜" eye bolts with nuts
- Four ⅜" locking washers
- Two 2" x 24" tow straps
- ½" rope, nylon or cotton, long enough to twice reach the ground from the tree branch you will be hanging the swing from
- Clear outdoor sealer
- Waterproof craft glue

TOOLS

- Saw
- Palm sander
- Drill
- ⅜" drill bit
- Crescent wrench
- Tape measure
- Clamps
- Ladder

TIME: 1 hour, plus dry time

LEVEL: Beginner

1. Cut two 24" x 5½" x ¾" pallet boards from the 5½" x ¾" pallet boards.

2. Cut two 11" x 3½" x ¾" pallet boards from the 3½" x ¾" pallet board.

3. Sand the boards well.

4. Join the 24" x 5½" x ¾" seat boards together with the 11" x 3½" x ¾" boards. Line up the two 24" boards next to each other, horizontally, then place the 11" boards underneath, perpendicularly, with one on each end. Hold them in place with a small clamp, then secure each of the 11" boards with eight 1¼" screws, four per seat board.

5. In each of the four swing seat corners, measure and mark 1½" in from the short sides of the seat and 2" in from the long sides of the seat.

6. Using a ⅜" drill bit, drill a hole on each of the marks made in the previous step.

7. Sand the swing seat again to make sure there are no wood splinters.

8. Finish as desired. I stained the seat and finished it with a good outdoor spar urethane clear coat.

9. To hang the swing, you need the eye bolts, nuts, washers, tow straps, and ropes.

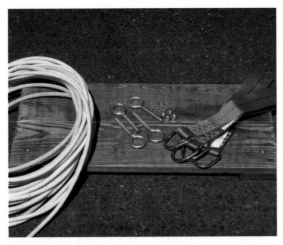

10. Put the eye bolts through the holes, with the eye on the top of the seat. Place a locking washer on the bolt side, and secure it with the nut. Use a crescent wrench to tighten the nut.

11. Hanging the swing is a two-person job. Please be safe—call a tree-cutting service if you do not have a safe way to hang the swing.

My husband used a tall ladder that I held. Place the tow straps around the branch, and then attach the rope to the straps using a fisherman's knot. We looked up how to tie the knots online.

12. Start a double eight knot on the rope end, about four feet from the ground.

13. Feed the rope through the eye bolts and then finish the double eight knot. Repeat on the other side of the swing.

help it hold. You can burn the end of nylon rope to prevent fraying.

14. Adjust the knot to adjust the height of the swing for your needs. Cotton rope knots hold better than nylon rope, but nylon rope will last longer. I used a little waterproof craft glue on the end of the cotton rope to

FALL

Fall is my favorite season, and I believe that Montana is at its very best in the fall. As a kid, I loved the start of the new school year, and that excitement continued throughout my 25 years as a teacher. The warm days and cooler nights, the changing colors of the autumn leaves, and watching football and volleyball games are all the things I adore about autumn. There are a variety of pallet projects in this section, each one created to help you enjoy the fall season to the fullest.

PORCH PUMPKIN PATCH

When I decorate for fall, I like to choose items that will work from September through November. This pumpkin patch is perfect for the entire autumn season, and it greets your guests throughout the fall. It is cheery and adds a great pop of fall color to your home. The pumpkins are grouped together, but can also easily be used separately as hanging signs or propped on a shelf or windowsill.

Note: The thickness of the pallet boards is not important for this project. However, the thinner boards are easier to cut. Also note that this pumpkin patch is sturdy enough to stand on its own. If you will be using it somewhere that gets a lot of wind, you may want to attach one more pallet 2" x 4" behind the back pumpkin to give it a more solid base.

SUPPLIES

- Two 48" x 5½" x ½" pallet boards
- Three 42" x 5½" x 1/2" pallet boards
- Three 42" x 3½" x ½" pallet boards

- Two 30" x 2" x 4" pallet runner boards
- Pencil
- 1" screws

- 1⅝" screws
- 2½" screws
- 3 yards of jute or hemp twine

- 3 feet of 20 gauge wire
- Outdoor paint
- Paintbrush
- Stencils

TOOLS

- Jigsaw, band saw, or scroll saw

- Palm sander
- Drill

- Wire cutters

TIME: 1½ hours, plus dry time   **LEVEL:** Beginner

1. Cut three 28" x 5½" x ½" boards and four 18" x 5½" x ½" boards from the 5½" x ½" pallet boards. Save the ends and scraps.

2. Cut three 32" x 3½" x ½" boards from the 42" x 3½" x ½" pallet boards. Save the ends and scraps.

3. Place the three 28" x 5½" x ½" boards next to each other and sketch a pumpkin. You can see that it took me a few tries to get a pumpkin that I like. Try to use up as much of the space as possible and use the straight edges of the board for the sides of the pumpkin. If you re-draw the pumpkin like I did, make sure to know which lines are your cutting lines.

4. Cut out the pumpkin using a jigsaw, band saw, or scroll saw. Because you are

cutting out the pieces individually, they are very easy to cut.

5. Using two of the end pieces saved from steps 1 and 2, join the pumpkin pieces together on the back by drilling six 1" screws into each "pumpkin" board, placing them diagonally from each other.

6. Using one of the scraps from cutting out the pumpkin boards, create a stem for the pumpkin. You can cut a stem from the scraps, but I always seems to find a stem shaped piece in the scraps. Attach it to the back of the pumpkin using one 1" screw.

7. Create two more pumpkins, one with the three 32" boards and a shorter, fatter one with the four 18" boards.

8. Sand the pumpkins and paint as desired. I painted them with yellow, bright orange, and darker orange paints, blending the colors while they were still wet. I used a buffalo check stencil and plaid stencil from Funky Junk's Old Sign Stencils to decorate two of the pumpkins (see Resources on page 124).

9. Sand and paint the two 30" x 2" x 4" pallet boards. I painted mine green.

10. Place one pumpkin on the back of one of the 2" x 4" boards, toward the end of the board. Secure it to the board with 1⅝" screws.

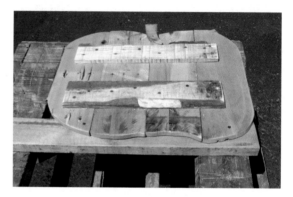

11. Turn over the board to the front and add another pumpkin to the opposite end of the board, securing it with 1⅝" screws. This pumpkin will be sandwiched between the two 2" x 4" boards. Screw two scrap boards to the 2" x 4" board, between the two pumpkins, as spacers.

12. Attach the second 2" x 4" board to the first 2" x 4" board, placing one end on top of the spacers and extending it past the second pumpkin. Use 2½" screws to secure it.

13. Place the third pumpkin on top of the top 2" x 4" board, in between the two other pumpkins. Secure it with 2½" screws.

14. Cut six pieces of jute, approximately 1'.

15. Cut three pieces of the 20 gauge wire, approximately 1'.

16. Tie two pieces of jute and one piece of wire to each pumpkin stem. Curl the wire around a pencil to create vine tendrils.

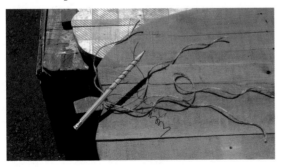

FIREWOOD CRATE

Friday nights in the fall are for friends, family, football, and bonfires. We recently built a fire pit in our backyard, but we needed some place to keep the wood scraps (mostly pallet pieces) that we use for bonfires. This great-looking lidded crate holds plenty of wood and helps keep it dry. If you live in a wet climate, this crate is large enough to hold and disguise a plastic storage container inside of it to protect wood from too much moisture. Keep the crate stocked with wood, and you will be ready for a bonfire at a moment's notice.

SUPPLIES

- Twenty-one 40" x 3½" x ⅜" pallet boards
- Sixteen 40" x 5½" x ¾" pallet boards
- 1⅝" screws
- 1¼" screws
- 3" stainless hinges
- Paint
- Paintbrush
- Stain
- Stencils

TOOLS

- Circular saw, jigsaw, or table saw
- Palm sander
- Drill
- Tape measure
- Clamps
- Countersink bit

TIME: 3 hours, plus dry time   **LEVEL:** Expert

1. Cut eight 16" x 3½" x ⅜" boards, two 18 ½" x 3 ½" x ⅜" boards, eleven 37¼ x 3½" x ⅜" boards, and four 22½" x 3½" x ⅜" boards from the 40" x 3½" x ⅜" pallet boards.

2. Cut eight 21" x 5½" x ¾" boards, eight 36" x 5½" x ¾" boards, and four 34⅝" x 5½" x ¾" boards from the 40" x 5½" x ¾" pallet boards.

3. Using a circular saw, jigsaw, or table saw, rip one of the 34⅝" x 5½" x ¾" boards down to 4½" wide for the bottom of the crate.

4. Join the 21" x 5½" x ¾" boards to the 36" x 5½" x ¾" boards at a right angle. It is easiest to join the boards together if you put the 21" board in the vice of a worktable. If you do not have a vice available, you can balance the 36" board on two 21" boards to join them together. Secure the 36" board to the 21" board using two 1⅝" screws at the right angle joint. Be sure to countersink the screws.

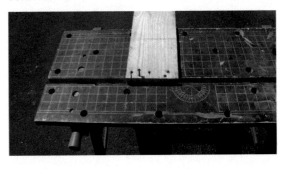

5. Repeat step 4 until you create eight Ls.

6. Join two Ls together to make a rectangle frame, drilling two 1⅝" screws into each corner. Join the remaining Ls to make a total of four rectangles.

7. On one of the rectangle frames (this will become the top of the crate), place a 22½" x 3½" x ⅜" board on the top edge of the short side for the top trim. Secure it in place using three 1¼" screws, drilling from the inside of the frame.

8. Repeat step 7 on the opposite short side of the same rectangle.

9. Secure two 37¼" x 3½" x ⅜" boards to the long sides of the same rectangle frame, screwing from the inside of the frame using four 1¼" screws, two on the ends and two evenly spaced in the middle.

10. On your work table, set the four rectangle frames up on their short ends. Place a 16" x 3½" x ⅜" board under the rectangle frames at the corner, flush against the edge of the boards and butted against the top trim board. This will be the vertical trim board and will join the rectangle frames together. Use a clamp to hold it in place.

11. Screw the vertical trim board to the rectangle frames using 1¼" screws, drilling from the inside of the box. Use two screws on each of the end rectangle frame boards, and one screw per board on the two middle frame boards.

12. Continue to add 16" x 3½" x ⅜" vertical trim boards to the corners to join the rectangle frames together, adding them to the shorter sides of the crate first and then to the longer sides.

13. Fit the three 34⅝" x 5½" x ¾" boards and the 34⅝" x 4½" x ¾" board into the bottom of the crate. Secure them into place using 1⅝" screws, two on each end of each board.

14. To further secure the bottom of the crate, screw two 1⅝" screws per side into the bottom boards along the front and back

sides of the crate, placing the screws approximately 12" apart.

15. Add the final four trim boards (the 22" x 3½" x ⅜" boards on the short sides and the 37¼" x 3½" x ⅜" boards on the long sides) along bottoms of the sides of the crate, securing them from the inside with 1¼" screws. Use three screws on the shorter sides and four screws on the longer sides.

16. Place one 37¼" x 3½" x ⅜" board on the open top of the crate, along one of the long sides. Secure to the crate using four evenly spaced 1⅝" screws.

17. Build the crate lid by joining the remaining six 37¼" x 3½" x ⅜" boards together with the two 18½" x 3½" x ⅜" boards; lay the two 18½" boards perpendicularly across the six longer boards, at opposite ends. For each of the 18½" boards, secure using two 1¼" screws on the end boards and one screw on the middle boards.

18. Using the 3" hinges placed about 6" from each side, attach the lid to the back top board added in step 16 with the screws that came with the hinge.

19. Finish as desired. I painted just the trim boards in a bright red. Using Waverly letter stencils, I stenciled FIREWOOD on top. When the paint was dry, I used a light golden pecan stain over the entire crate. I did not use a clear sealer because I want the finish to age with time.

PALLET POINTERS
VARIATIONS

This crate makes a great indoor trunk, as well. Use it at the end of a bed for a blanket chest or in the family room for a coffee table with storage. Add slow, soft closing hinges to use the crate as a toy box. If using it as a toy box, drill three or four 1" air holes in the back of the crate for extra safety. Outside, the crate works well to store outdoor furniture cushions or sports equipment.

RAKE AND LEAF-BAG CART

When we moved into an old schoolhouse a few years ago, we were thrilled to have huge, 85-year-old trees. We love the trees and the shade they provide in the summer. But, come fall, we have a lot of leaves to rake. This rake and leaf-bag cart makes the job a little easier. It is easy to roll to the area that needs raking, and the leaf bag is easy to fill with the convenient holder that keeps the bag open. There is a space to hold two rakes, because raking autumn leaves with someone else is always better.

SUPPLIES

- Four 40" x 5½" x ¾" pallet boards
- Four 40" x 3½" x ¾" pallet boards
- Four 48" x 2" x 4" pallet boards

- Pencil

- 1⅝" screws
- 2" screws
- 1¼" screws
- 5"-diameter, non-swiveling casters, with an overall height of 6½"
- ⅛" x ¾" fender washers
- Stain

TOOLS

- Saw
- Palm sander
- Drill
- 1½" hole saw or paddle bit
- 1⅛" paddle bit
- Tape measure
- Clamps
- Countersink bit

TIME: 2½ hours, plus dry time **LEVEL:** Intermediate

1. Cut two 34" x 3½" x ¾" boards, two 15" x 3½" x ¾" boards, and one 13½" x 3½" x ¾" board from the 40" x 3½" x ¾" pallet boards.

2. Cut two 28" x 5½" x ¾" boards, one 15" x 5½" x ¾" board, and one 13½" x 5½" x ¾" board from the 40" x 5½" x ¾" pallet boards.

3. Cut two 42" x 2" x 4" boards, two 34¼" x 2" x 4" boards, and two 15" x 2" x 4" boards from the 48" x 2" x 4" pallet boards.

4. Sand all of the boards.

5. On the 42"- and 34¼"-long 2" x 4" boards, mark 2" from one end on each board. On the opposite end of the 42" boards, mark 7¾" inches.

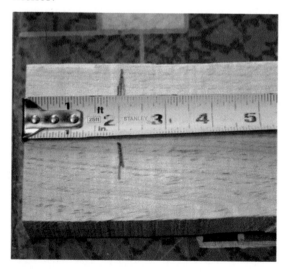

6. On both 34" x 3½" x ¾" boards and 28" x 5½" x ¾" boards, mark 19" from one end. To make sure my marks were even, I marked two boards at one time.

7. Lay one 42" x 2" x 4" board and one 34¼" x 2" x 4" on your work table. Place one 34" x 3½" x ¾" board perpendicularly on top of the 2" x 4" boards, with the top edge of the 34" board at the 2" marks. The 19" mark on the 34" board should hit the outside edge of the 34¼" x 2" x 4".

8. Place one of the 28" x 5½" x ¾" perpendicularly on top of the 2" x 4" boards, aligning its outer edge with the 7¾" mark on the 42" x 2" x 4" board and with the end of the 34¼" x 2" x 4" board. The 19" mark on the 28" board should hit the outer edge of the 34" board.

9. Secure all four boards with two 1⅝" screws at each of the four intersections. Align the screws diagonally.

10. Repeat steps 7 through 9 to create a second side.

11. Rest the sides on the 2" edges of the 34¼" boards, then join the sides by placing one of the 15" x 3½" boards flat against the 42" boards, at the same level as the 34" x 3½" x ¾" boards. Make sure there are still 2" extending above the 15" x 3½" board— these 2" pegs are the leaf bag holders at the top of the cart. Secure the 15" board with 1⅝" screws. Screw one screw into each side

for stability, and then add a second screw to each side.

12. Secure the 15" x 5½" x ¾" board flat against the bottom part of the 42" boards at the same level as the 28" x 5½" x ¾", using two 1⅝" screws per side. Screw in one screw on each side to stabilize the board, before adding the second screw.

13. Turn the cart over and secure the 13½" x 3½" x ¾" and the 13½" x 5½" x ¾" boards to the supporting 2" x 4" boards at the same heights as the 15" board attached in steps 11. Use 1⅝" screws, two on each end of each board.

14. Turn the cart upside down and lay the two 15" x 2" x 4" boards flat on the ends of the 5½" x ¾" boards. Secure the 15" x 2" x 4" boards with one 2" screw at each end. Be sure to pre-drill so that you do not split the ¾" edge on the 5½" boards.

15. Secure the two casters to the outside edges of the 15" x 2" x 4" boards, using the washers and 1¼" screws.

16. Turn the cart upright. Measure and mark 3½" in from the 7½" handles that extend from the end of the 34¼" x 2" x 4" boards.

17. On the remaining 15" x 3½" x ¾" board, measure and mark the 5" and 10" points in the middle of the board. Using the 1½" hole saw drill bit, drill holes where you made marks.

18. Secure the inside edge of the board to the cart handle at the 3½" mark made in step 16 using 1⅝" screws. Use a clamp, if necessary, to hold the board in place.

19. On the 15" x 2" x 4" caster boards, measure and mark at 4½" and at 9".

20. Use the 1⅛" paddle drill bit to drill a hole about ½" deep to hold the rake handles in place.

21. On the top end with the bag holder pegs, measure and mark 10" in from both sides. Screw a 1¼" screw at both marks, screwing them in enough to remain stable, but not so much that the screws come through the other side. These screws are used to hold the drawstring of the leaf bag.

22. Finish as desired. I stained the cart with Minwax's Special Walnut Stain. I did not use a clear sealer on the cart because it will be stored in my garage when not in use.

BACK-TO-SCHOOL BOOKSHELF

As a former teacher, I love books, and I believe it is important to have books in the home. When my children were school-aged, they always had bookshelves in their rooms filled with great books. This bookshelf is a smaller sized bookcase that fits in little spaces and rooms. Even though it is small, it holds plenty of books (and décor items), and will inspire even the reluctant reader to read.

SUPPLIES

- Six 48" x 5½" x ¾" pallet boards

(Note: two of my boards were 5¼" wide rather than 5½". I used these two boards for the middle shelves. Either 5½" or 5¼" will work for the middle shelves, and I will refer to them as 5½" boards for ease of distinguishing boards from each other, but you will notice in the photos that the middle shelves are set back a bit from the edge.)

- Six 48" x 3⅜" x ½" pallet boards

- Two 48" x 2" x 4" pallet runner boards

- One notched 48" x 2" x 4" pallet runner board

- 2" screws
- 1⅝" screws
- 1¼" screws

- Paint
- Paintbrush
- Stain
- Clear sealer

TOOLS

- Saw
- Palm sander
- Drill
- Tape measure
- Clamps
- Countersink bit

TIME: 2 hours, plus dry time   **LEVEL:** Beginner

1. Cut four 42" x 5½" x ¾" boards, two 20½" x 5½" x ¾" boards, and six 19" x 5½" x ¾" boards from the 48" x 5½" x ¾" pallet boards.

2. Cut three 19" x 2" x 4" boards, four 9" x 2" x 4" boards, two 42" x 2" x 4" boards, and four 8½" x 2" x 4" boards from the 48" x 2" x 4" pallet boards.

3. Cut six 42" x 3⅜" x ½" boards from the 48" x 3⅜" x ½" pallet boards.

4. Find and mark the middle point of the notch on the notched 2" x 4" board. Most notches are 9" long, so you would mark at 4½".

5. Measure and mark 19" on the notched pallet, placing the 9½" tape measure point on the center of the notch mark made in the

previous step. Cut the board to be 19" long, with the notch centered in the middle.

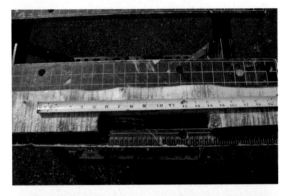

6. Sand all of the boards.

7. Start by making two "frames" with the 19"- and 8½"-long 2" x 4" boards. (One frame will be made with the 19" notched 2" x 4" board.) Sandwich two 8½" x 2" x 4" boards between two 19" x 2" x 4" boards. Secure with 2" screws, two per joint.

8. Set the two frames on their shorter sides, making sure the open part of the notch is not facing the middle. Join the frames together with two 42" x 5½" x ¾" boards, using 1⅝" screws. Use four screws for each board, two per end.

9. Turn the shelf over and attach the remaining two 42" x 5½" x ¾" boards to the other side.

10. Secure the two 20½" x 5½" x ¾" boards to the top, unnotched frame of the bookshelf, using 1⅝" screws, two on each end of each board.

11. Attach two of the 19" x 5½" x ¾" boards inside the bottom frame of the bookshelf, using 1⅝" screws, two on each end of each board.

12. Along the inner walls of the bookshelf, measure and mark 11" and at 22½" from the bottom of each wall to note the position for the shelf brace boards. Make the marks wide and straight.

13. Place the top edges of the 9" x 2" x 4" boards on the marks and clamp in place.

14. Secure the shelf brace boards with two 1⅝" screws per each board, screwing in from the outside of the shelf.

15. Paint and stain the bookshelf at this point; it easier to get in all of the corners now, rather than when the shelf is completed. I painted the outside of the shelf in a dark green that I custom mixed, and then I stained everything with a dark walnut stain.

16. When the bookshelf is dry, add the four remaining 19" x 5½" x ¾" boards as the middle shelves, placing them on the 2" x 4" braces and securing them with two 1⅝" screws per each end of each board.

17. Place the six 42" x 3⅜" x ½" boards on the back of the bookshelf. Use a clamp if necessary to hold them in place and square up the bookshelf. Screw the back boards into the 2" x 4" frame boards, using two 1¼" screws per board, one screw on each end. I always like to screw in the four corner screws first, before the other screws.

18. Finish with a clear sealer of choice.

PALLET POINTERS
VARIATIONS

Once you know how to make a pallet bookshelf, you can vary the basic construction and size to create a piece that works well for you. You can make a much larger shelf using longer boards. Be sure that the middle shelf boards are sturdy and rigid so that they do not sag. You can vary the spacing on the shelves, adding more shelves that are closer together (perfect for paperback books). Make a shorter, wider shelf with only one middle board to use as a television stand.

This shelf also works hard in other rooms. Use it in the bathroom to store extra towels, toiletries, and toilet paper. In the kitchen, it holds cookbooks and canisters and dishes. Put it to work in a mudroom to store shoes and a basket with hats and mittens, or use it in the laundry room to hold cleaning supplies. When you see how easy the bookshelf is to make, you will want to build one for every room of the home.

HARVEST TABLE AND BENCH

Harvest tables date back to the early American colonists. Typically, they are longer, narrower, and more simply crafted tables that are used to display and share a bountiful harvest in the autumn. This modified pallet version is not quite as long as most harvest tables are. It is narrower than standard kitchen tables and is made to look like something that a farmer would perhaps put together in the barn with extra boards. One bench seat matches the table style and two found chairs create a farmhouse feel. The table provides seating for four, and the table legs are set in so that chairs can be added to the ends if needed.

SUPPLIES

- Five 60" x 2" x 4" pallet runner boards
- Two 48" x 3½" x ¾" pallet boards
- Two 48" x 5½" x ¾" pallet boards
- One 3½" x ¾" pallet board, at least 8" long (this can be a scrap piece from another project)

- Two 48" x 2" x 4" pallet runner boards
- Six 30" x 5½" x ¾" pallet boards
- Five 30" x 3½" x ¾" pallet boards

- Pencil
- 2½" screws
- 1⅝" screws
- 1¼" nails
- Paint

- Paintbrush
- Stain
- T-shirt rags
- Coconut oil or clear finish of choice

TOOLS

- Saw
- Palm sander

- Drill
- Tape measure

- Clamps
- Countersink bit

TIME: 3 hours, plus dry time   **LEVEL:** Intermediate

1. Cut four 29" x 2" x 4" boards, four 17" x 2" x 4" boards, four 6" x 2" x 4" boards, and four 12" x 2" x 4" boards from the 48" x 2" x 4" pallet runner boards.

2. Cut one 8" x 3½" x ¾" board from one of the 30" x 3½" x ¾" pallet boards.

3. Trim the ends off of the 30"-long 5½" and 3½" boards so that the ends are straight and even. The easiest way to do this is to cut about ⅛" off of each end, making sure that the boards are all trimmed to the same length.

4. Trim the ends off of the 48"-long 5½" and 3½" boards so that ends are straight

and even. Make sure that the boards are trimmed to the same length.

5. Sand all of the boards.

6. To make one of the two sets of table leg bases, use a clamp to hold the 12" x 2" x 4" board between two 29" x 2" x 4" legs, creating a U shape.

7. Secure the legs to the 12" cross piece by drilling two 2½" screws into each end. Countersink the screws.

8. Place the bottom 12" x 2" x 4" leg brace between the legs. Use the 6" x 2" x 4" boards as a jig to set the 12" brace in place (the 6" boards will be reused as cross braces later), with the 6" boards underneath the 12" brace. Hold the brace in place with a clamp.

9. Secure the brace to the legs using 2½" screws, two per each side.

10. Repeat steps 6 through 9 to create the second set of table leg bases.

11. Make the bench leg bases using the same method as the table bases, using the 17" legs and the 6" cross braces. Instead of using a jig to place the 6" cross braces, measure 3" up from the bottom of the bench legs and place the bottom edge of the 6" cross brace at the 3" mark.

12. On the 48" x 2" x 4" boards (the table apron boards), measure and mark 10" in on either side.

13. Place the outside edge of the top of one of the table leg bases on either of the 10" marks, keeping the top of the table base flush with the edge of the apron. Use the second 48" x 2" x 4" board under the leg base to hold it steady. Secure from the inside of the leg with two 2½" screws placed diagonally.

14. Repeat step 13 with the second set of legs, on the other 10" mark.

15. Add the second 48" x 2" x 4" apron to the other side of the table leg bases.

16. On the outside of the apron, further secure the leg bases by screwing in two 2½" screws diagonally into the top of the legs. Feel underneath the apron to be sure to place the screws on the opposite diagonal as the screws screwed in on the other side.

17. For the table top, place the 30"-long 5½" and 3½" boards horizontally on top of the table apron boards, alternating between the two sized boards. Make sure to have an equal overhang on both sides and the ends.

18. Secure the table top boards to the 2" x 4" table aprons using 1⅝" screws. Use four screws per each 5½" board, and two screws on each 3½" board. I move the board next to

the one I am currently securing to better see where I need to screw. Be sure to countersink the screws.

19. Sand the table top well before finishing.

20. Join the bench leg bases together with the two 48" x 3½" x ¾" bench apron boards, using two 1⅝" screws placed diagonally at each corner.

21. Join the two 48" x 5½" x ¾" boards together for the bench top by screwing the

8" x 3½" x ¾" board in the middle of the 48" boards. Secure using 1¼" screws.

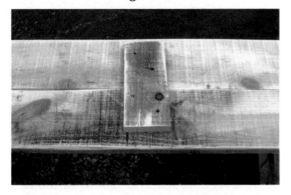

22. Secure the bench top to the bench leg bases using four 1⅝" screws per end.

23. Add two more 1⅝" screws to the middle of the bench top, screwing them down through the ¾" apron edge. I used a clamp to hold the boards tightly to the apron.

24. Finish the table and bench as desired. I used a teal color, which is a color I love for fall, on the bases, and then dark walnut stain over all of it.

25. Use a protective clear sealer on the table and bench top. I used coconut oil because it is food safe and creates a water-resistant finish. I keep a jar of coconut oil in my kitchen for cooking and in my workshop for a clear finish. It will soak into the wood and harden over time. It is easy to polish the table with more coconut oil when needed.

LET'S TALK PAINT COLORS

I often get asked on my blog, *Beyond the Picket Fence*, what a particular color is. And while I am happy to answer and let people know, I do always encourage those inquiring to go and peruse the paint chips at their local hardware store. Colors do not always translate well online.

When picking colors, think about which colors you love. Look to your wardrobe and nature for inspiration. I love the water and will always have some form of aqua blue or turquoise in my home. What are your favorite flower colors?

Use your favorite neutral color (gray, black, white, beige, navy, or brown) in several areas in your home, and then add pops of color with small furniture pieces, wall art, blankets, and pillows. This makes it easy to change colors when you want to, or to match the seasons. I use a little more orange and yellow in the fall, red in the winter, and green in the spring and summer.

Paint is forgiving. You can always repaint a piece if the color is not working for you. You can also warm up a paint color by using a light stain over it with a yellow base—look for golden oak and golden pecan. To darken and deepen color, use dark stains over the paint.

Purchase a color wheel at a craft store and keep it with you to find complementary and corresponding colors.

Remember to choose colors that speak to *you*, rather than worrying about color trends.

WINTER

Living in Montana during the winter is not for the faint of heart. We have long stretches of days with subzero temperatures and many inches of snow to shovel. But, because we choose to live here, I embrace winter. We enjoy skiing and snowboarding, ice skating, and sledding. I love when I can spend a cold day curling up under a warm blanket, reading a book, and sipping hot cocoa or tea. And, my favorite holiday, Christmas, is in the winter. I like to spend a few weeks decorating my home inside and out for Christmas. The pallet projects in this section celebrate winter and help make our longest season a bit more cheery.

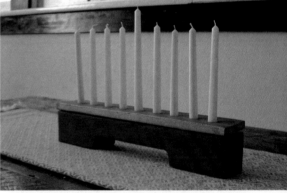

HOT COCOA CART

A steamy mug of hot cocoa is the perfect way to warm up on a cold winter's day. A cart stocked full of cocoa-making supplies plus some delicious extras makes the hot chocolate experience all the more enjoyable. Fill jars with different varieties of cocoa mix, marshmallows, candy canes, and chocolate bars. Store favorite cocoa mugs and saucers on the cart, along with a dish towel or cloth napkins. Add hot water or milk when you are ready for something warm to drink, and you are all set for a cozy cup of cocoa. The removable tray makes serving family and guests easy. This piece also works well for a bar cart, tea cart, or lunch cart.

SUPPLIES

- One small 32" x 20½" pallet

- Three 42" x 2" x 4" pallet runner boards

- Four 48" x 3½" x ¾" pallet boards
- Two scrap 2" x 4" boards, at least 20" long
- Three 5½" x ¾" pallet boards, at least 24" long
- One 1" diameter wood dowel, at least 17" long
- Pencil

- Two 3" swivel casters
- 2" screws
- 1⅝" screws
- 1" screws
- ¾" #8 truss head screws
- 30" of ¾" plumber's tape
- Clear sealer
- Paintbrush

TOOLS

- Jigsaw or circular saw
- Palm sander
- Drill

- Tape measure
- Clamps
- Straightedge

- Rubber mallet
- Tin snips

TIME: 4 hours, plus dry time   **LEVEL:** Expert

Refer to the following diagram when building the cocoa cart.

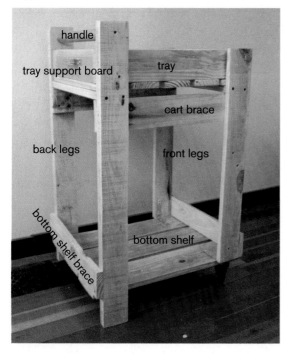

1. Using your preferred pallet board removal method, remove the two back boards from the small pallet.

2. On the top of the pallet, draw a straight line on the top boards along one outside edge of the middle runner board.

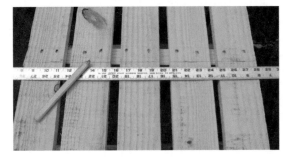

3. Using a jigsaw or circular saw, cut along the line drawn in step 2. You will use the piece with two runner boards to make the tray.

4. Cut two 35" x 2" x 4" pallet runner boards for the back legs from the 42" x 2" x 4" pallet runner boards.

5. Cut two 28" x 3½" x ¾" boards for the front legs and two 21" x 3½" x ¾" boards for cart braces from the 48" x 3½" x ¾" pallet boards. With the leftover pieces, cut two 17" x 3½" x ¾" boards, one 19½" x 3½" x ¾" board, and one 18½" x 3½" x ¾" board.

6. Cut two 13½" x 2" x 4" boards from the scrap 2" x 4" boards.

7. Cut three 22½" x 5½" x ¾" boards from the 5½" x ¾" pallet boards.

8. Cut the 1" dowel to be 17" long, if it isn't already.

9. Sand all of the wood pieces.

10. Finish the tray by adding the 13½" x 2" x 4" pieces to the open ends of the pallet piece cut off in step 3. Secure the 13½" boards in place with two 2" screws on each corner.

11. Join the 28" x 3½" x ¾" front legs together with the 18½" x 3½" x ¾" bottom shelf brace board. Prop up both 28" boards on their ¾" edges and place the 18" board flat across, perpendicularly, so it is flush against the bottom edges of the 28" boards. Secure the brace board with two 1⅝" screws per end.

12. On the top end of the front legs, measure and mark 4½" down from the edge.

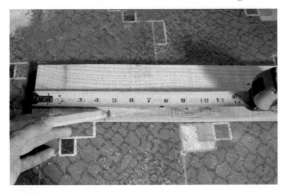

13. Place the 17" x 3½" x ¾" tray support board perpendicularly between the front legs at the 4½" mark, lying on its edge. The top edge of the tray support board should be on the 4½" mark, leaving a 4½" space above

the tray support board. Hold the board in place with a clamp.

14. Secure the tray support board in place with two 1⅝" screws per side, drilled through the outside of the front legs.

15. Measure and mark 3¾" down from the end of the two 35" x 2" x 4" back leg boards. I measured and marked both boards at the same time, which is a great way to make sure your marks are in the same place.

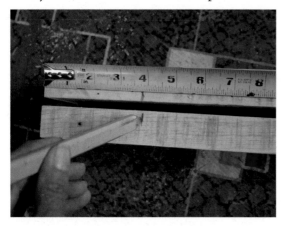

16. Join the 35" x 2" x 4" back legs together with the 19½" x 3½" x ¾" bottom shelf brace board by placing the brace board flat across the back legs. Place the bottom edge of the brace board on the 3¾" mark made in the previous step, leaving a 3¾" space below the brace. Secure with two 1⅝" screws per end of the brace board.

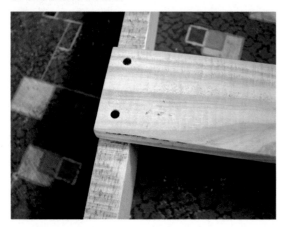

17. On the top end of the back legs, measure and mark 8" down from the edge. Place the 17" x 3½" x ¾" tray support board between the back legs at the 8" mark. The top edge

of the tray support board should be on the 8" mark, leaving an 8" space above the tray support board. Hold the board in place with a clamp.

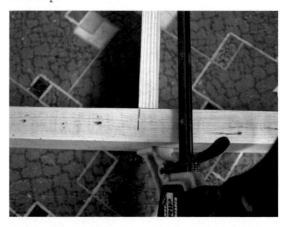

18. Secure the tray support board to the back legs with two 2" screws per side, drilled through the outside edge of the back legs.

19. Turn the front legs upside down so that the bottom shelf brace board faces upward, and balance the front legs on the two scrap 2" x 4" boards to raise them up.

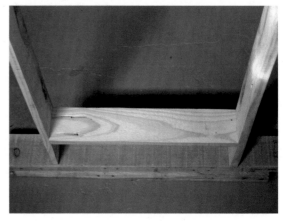

20. Turn the back legs upside down, with the bottom shelf brace facing upward, and set them across from the front legs. Carefully balance the 22½" x 5½" x ¾" boards for the bottom shelf on the bottom shelf brace boards between the sets of legs. The bottom shelf boards should measure 17" across to create a 22½" x 17" bottom shelf.

21. Secure the bottom shelf boards, starting with the outside boards, by screwing 1⅝" screws through the 22½" x 5½" x ¾" shelf boards into the ¾" edge of the bottom shelf brace. Use clamps as necessary.

22. Add the two casters to the front of the cart using the ¾" #8 truss head screws. Be sure to predrill the holes through the 22½"

shelf boards, as these are thicker screws that will crack the wood if you do not predrill.

23. In between the front and back legs, place the 21" x 3½" x ¾" cart brace boards under the tray support boards, flat against the legs. Secure in place with two 1" screws per side, 4 screws per cart brace board.

24. Center the 17" wood dowel handle 1½" from the top edge of the upper part of the back legs. Secure it with two 2" screws, one per side.

25. Finish as desired. I wanted an industrial look, as if this cart might have been used in a factory somewhere, so I left the wood natural and finished it with a clear coat of Minwax Polyacrylic in a satin finish.

26. Using the tins snips, cut four 7" pieces of plumber's tape.

27. Fold two of the 7" pieces of plumber's tape in half, using the rubber mallet.

28. Open up the tape to make an L. Hammer the ends down so there are no sharp edges sticking up. Secure the Ls to the bottom shelf and the front legs, using the ¾" #8 truss screws, 4 screws for each L.

29. From the remaining two pieces of plumber's tape, shape handles for the tray.

Hammer the ends down with the rubber mallet so there are no sharp edges.

30. Secure the plumber's tape handles to the ends of the tray using the ¾" #8 truss screws, centering the handles on the ends of the board.

HOW TO GET DIFFERENT STYLES WITH YOUR PALLET WOOD PIECES

I always include "Finish as desired" in each set of directions because we all have different tastes. But there are certain elements that will help you achieve a particular look that you may want.

Industrial: Use metal elements such as plumber's tape, galvanized pipe, and joiner plates. Keep wood natural for a more urban feel or stain for a more rustic industrial look. Big casters added to furniture pieces enhance the industrial feel.

Eclectic boho: Paint wood in a variety of bright colors, such as turquoise, red, orange, bright green, and bright yellow. Use natural elements, such as hemp twine and cotton rope. Add boho design with paisley and mandala style stencils.

Farmhouse: Paint farmhouse pieces white, and sand some of the paint off for a chippy look. Keep parts of the wood unpainted. Add number stencils or simple words to things with black paint. If you want to use some color, use light pastels such as mint green or butter yellow. Rusty metal elements work well to add a farmhouse touch to items.

Modern: Sand wood well for a sleeker, modern look. Use glossy paint in white, black, or gray. Use shiny, polished metal hardware (handles, brackets, etc.). Geometric design stencils work well with a modern style.

Rustic: Keep wood rougher and stain rather than paint the wood. Use antique bronze finish or rust for metal elements. Jute rope and leather elements add rustic style. Buffalo check, plaid, and kilim design stencils create an instant rustic look.

CHRISTMAS TREE CRATE

They say necessity is the mother of invention, and that would be true for this Christmas tree crate. When we bought an 8'-tall artificial tree at an after-Christmas sale a few years ago, we had no idea that we would be moving into a new home with 12' ceilings. Not wanting to purchase a taller tree, I decided to come up with a unique way to add a little more height to our existing tree. This crate not only adds more height to the tree, but it acts as a fantastic, rustic "tree skirt." It will hold and hide either an artificial tree stand or a tree stand for a live tree. It is also a great solution for keeping a tree up and away from little fingers and pets.

SUPPLIES

- Eight 48" x 5½" x ½" (or ¾") pallet boards
- Two 2" x 4" pallet runner boards
- One 3½" x ¾" pallet board
- 1¼" screws
- Paint
- Paintbrush
- Stencils
- Clear paste wax

TOOLS

- Saw
- Palm sander
- Drill
- Tape measure
- Clamps

TIME: 1 hour, plus dry time   **LEVEL:** Beginner

1. Cut twelve 22½" x 5½" x ½" boards, two 20¾" x 5½" x ½" boards, and two 18½" x 5½" x ½" boards.

2. Cut four 16" x 2" x 4" runner boards.

3. Cut two 22½" x 3½" x ¾" boards.

4. Sand all of the boards.

5. Make one side by placing three of the 22½" x 5½" x ½" boards on top of two of the 16" x 2" x 4" boards. Align the 2" x 4"s with to be flush with the short edges of the 22½" boards and with the bottom of the crate side. There will be a gap between the 2" x 4"s and the top of the crate side.

6. Secure the boards with 1¼" screws, drilling two through the end of each 5½" board.

7. Repeat steps 5 and 6 to make a second crate side.

8. Measure and mark 8" up from the bottom of the 2" x 4" boards on each side of the crates.

9. Place the 22½" x 3½" x ¾" board across the 2" x 4" boards, lining up the top edge of the 3½" board on the 8" mark.

10. Secure the board in place with 1¼" screws, two per end of the board.

11. Repeat steps 9 and 10 on the other crate side you made in step 7.

12. Join the two sides together by setting the sides up on their edges and placing a 22½" x 5½" x ½" across the bottom edge, flush with the bottom corners. Secure the 5½" board in place by screwing two 1¼" screws into each end of the 2" x 4" board.

13. Repeat step 12 on the other side of the crate. Use a clamp if necessary to square up the four sides. I did not need to use a clamp.

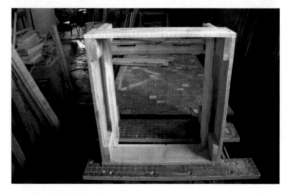

14. Fill in the sides with the other 22½" x 5½" x ½" boards. Secure the boards into the 2" x 4"s using 1¼" screws, two per end of the boards.

15. Place the remaining 5½" boards on the inside braces created in steps 8 through 10, placing the shorter 18½" boards on the ends where the 2" x 4" boards are.

16. Secure the boards in place with 1¼" screws, two per end of the boards, screwed into the 3½" x ¾" braces.

17. Finish the crate as desired. I used two stencils from Funky Junk's Old Sign Stencils (see Resources on page 124).

I placed them in different ways, sometimes stenciling off the edge of the crate. I stenciled some numbers as well. I used a clear paste wax to finish the crate to bring out the natural beauty of the wood.

(see Resources on page 124).

PALLET POINTERS
VARIATIONS

There are many different ways you can finish the tree crate to personalize it and fit your holiday décor. Paint it to look like a giant present and add actual ribbon, using a staple gun to hold the ribbon in place. Tie a big bow around the tree trunk. Sand the crate well and paint it a glossy white for a more sleek and modern look. Add locking casters to the bottom of the crate to make it even taller and easier to move. This crate looks wonderful on a front porch with a live tree in it. Use the crate in the off-season to store boxes of ornaments and other holiday décor.

STOCKING HANGER AND SHELF

The stockings were hung by the chimney with care...But, wait, what if your home doesn't have a fireplace? That was the problem we faced when we moved into our new home that did not have a fireplace and mantel. This stocking hanger is a great-looking solution to the no fireplace problem, and it has a small shelf or mantel, perfect for decorating. It can easily hang three, four, or five stockings, and you can simply alter the lengths of the boards to make a longer shelf to hang more than five stockings. This shelf also looks good hanging in an entryway or a child's room or even above a bed as a headboard with quilts and blankets hanging from the hooks.

SUPPLIES

- Eight 42" x 3½" x ½" (or ⅜") pallet boards
- One 42" x 5½" x ¾" pallet board
- One 48" x 2" x 4" pallet runner board

- 1" screws
- 1¼" screws
- Paint
- Paintbrush
- Stain
- 5 coat hooks
- 2 heavy-duty D-rings

TOOLS

- Miter saw
- Palm sander
- Drill
- Tape measure
- Clamp
- Countersink bit

TIME: 1½ hours, plus dry time   **LEVEL:** Intermediate

1. Cut three 36" x 3½" x ⅜" boards and three 10⅛" x 3½" x ⅜" boards from the 42" x 3½" x ½" pallet boards.

2. Cut one 36" x 5½" x ¾" board from the 42" x 5½" x ¾" pallet board.

3. Cut three 8½" x 2" x 4" pallet runner boards from the 2" x 4" boards.

4. Sand all of the boards.

5. Because I wanted the back wall boards painted and the rest of the shelf boards stained, I painted the three 36" x 3½" x ⅜" boards before assembling the shelf.

6. When the paint is dry, place the three 36" x 3½" x ⅜" boards face down on top of two 10⅛" x 3½" x ⅜" boards, with the two 10⅛" boards flush against the short ends of the 36" boards. Hold the boards in place with a small clamp and secure with one 1"

screw at the end of each 36" board, drilled in through the back.

7. Turn the shelf back board over and add the third 10⅛" board to the middle of the 36" boards, centered at the 18" mark, securing it in place with two 1" screws screwed in from the front.

8. To create the shelf braces, use a miter saw to cut the three 8½" x 2" x 4" boards into trapezoids with a 30-degree angle on one end and a 60-degree angle on the other end. After the cuts have been made, the long side of the trapezoid should still measure 8½" and the short side should be 5½" long.

9. Place the 36" x 5½" x ¾" shelf board along the top edge of the stocking hanger shelf, resting it on its ¾" edge. Hold one of the trapezoid braces in place so that the 30-degree angle touches the underside edge of the 5½" shelf and the 60-degree angle touches the 10⅛" board. Draw a line where the bottom of the brace touches the 10⅛" x 3½" board.

10. Secure the trapezoid brace to the 10⅛" board with two 1¼" screws, screwed through the front of the brace. Be sure to countersink the screws.

11. Repeat steps 9 and 10 with the other three trapezoid braces.

12. Secure the 36" x 5½" x ¾" shelf board in place by screwing two 1" screws into the top of each trapezoid brace, countersinking the screws.

13. Secure the top shelf board to the back board by screwing two 1" screws from the top of the shelf into the ⅜" back boards.

14. Sand the shelf again, especially the front edges of the braces that may hang over the shelf just a bit or be a little sharp.

15. Evenly space the coat hooks on the bottom edge of the stocking hanger back board. If you are using five hooks, place three of them under the braces as pictured. If you are using four hooks, place the hooks on the back boards only, not under the braces. If you are using three hooks, place one under each brace.

16. Stain the entire stocking hanger, even the hooks. I did not use a clear sealer on this piece because the stain acts as a sealer and protectant.

17. Add two heavy-duty D-rings to the back with 1" screws. If you are permanently hanging the shelf, consider screwing two screws through the back board of the shelf and directly into the wall.

PERSONALIZING STOCKINGS

I like to change up and personalize our stockings each year. You can start with basic stockings from the store or make your own. Create different cuffs for the stockings by sewing (or even hot gluing) a tube made out of scrap fabrics, tablecloths, vintage quilts, or chenille bedspreads. Add trim and fringe with hot glue. I like to use curtain clips to hang the stockings. There are lots of different ways to identify who each stocking belongs to. Tie on wood, metal, or cork initial letters from the craft store. You can use small chalkboard tags, wood branch slices painted with names, or a nice Christmas gift tag. Small objects from the dollar store that identify who the stocking belongs to also can be tied on to the curtain clip. Use items such as a fishing bobber, a small toy ball, a paintbrush, etc. Christmas ornaments make unique stocking name tags as well.

MENORAH

Growing up, I lived next to a rabbi, and each Chanukah I would be hired to polish all of the silver for the upcoming celebrations. The menorah was beautiful, but it was a challenge to polish each intricate candle cup. This menorah is a bit simpler than the one I polished, but just as beautiful, and it is kosher. In order for a menorah to be kosher, the candles or lights need to all be in a straight row, and the eight candles should be the same height. The middle candle, the *shamash*, should be slightly taller. You should use candles that will burn for at least 1½ hours. Whether you celebrate Chanukah or another holiday, this very easy project makes a beautiful candleholder for any occasion.

SUPPLIES

- One 48"-long 2" x 4" notched pallet runner board
- One 3½" x ¾" pallet board, at least 20" long
- Pencil
- Nine 10" taper candles
- Wood glue
- Four 1¼" finish nails
- Paint
- Paintbrush

TOOLS

- Saw
- Palm sander
- Drill
- ¾" paddle wood bit
- Tape measure
- Clamps
- Straightedge
- Hammer

TIME: 1 hour, plus dry time   **LEVEL:** Beginner

1. Measure and mark 5½" from each outside edge of one of the notches on the 2" x 4" pallet runner board.

Cut the board on these marks to make a 20"-long piece.

2. Using one of the notched pallet pieces to measure, make a mark on the 3½" x ¾" pallet board.

Cut the 3½" board on this line.

3. Generously apply glue to one side of one of the notched pallet boards and join it to the other notched board, using clamps to hold them together. Let the glue dry for several hours or overnight.

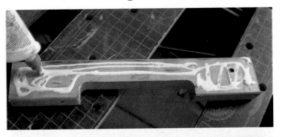

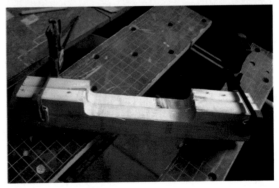

4. Sand the unnotched side of the joined pieces well and then attach the 20" x 3½" x

¾" to the top, using two 1¼" finishing nails on each end.

5. Thoroughly sand the candleholder.

6. On the top of the menorah, find the middle at the 1¾" mark, and using a straightedge, draw a light pencil line lengthwise down the middle. Mark nine dots along the line, marking every 2".

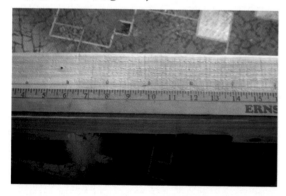

7. Using the ¾" paddle bit, drill a hole at each mark made in step 6.

8. To create a uniform hole depth, I used a scrap piece of wood that I marked with a pencil line in the first hole I drilled. I then used this to check the hole depth of each hole. My holes for the eight Chanukah candles were approximately 3/4" deep. The hole for the middle *shamash* candle should be a bit taller, so drill this hole only ⅜" to ½" deep.

9. Drill holes on each mark create nine candle holes.

10. Paint as desired. I used a metallic copper paint on the top piece and a dark blue on the bottom.

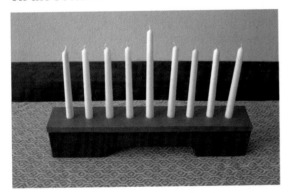

PALLET POINTERS

THE HISTORY OF THE MENORAH

The menorah is used during the Jewish celebration of Chanukah, also known as the Festival of Lights. The eight lights represent the miracle of the eight days that the Jews were able to burn oil for the rededication of the Temple, even though they only had enough oil to burn for a few hours. The middle candle represents the servant and it is used to light the other candles. The candles are lit from left to right. One new candle is lit each night for eight days, along with the previously lit candles. Chanukah is celebrated on different days each year because the Jewish calendar is lunar, but it is almost always celebrated in December.

CHRISTMAS TREE ORNAMENTS

Decorating the Christmas tree is one of my favorite holiday traditions. I love pulling out old ornaments from the past and remembering who they are from or why they were chosen. I also enjoy decorating with new ornaments each year, choosing a different theme. But, because I don't want to spend money on new ornaments every year, I typically make them. These simple pallet ornaments are quick to make and are definitely in the budget, because they are made from free pallet wood scraps.

SUPPLIES

- Pallet scraps from 3½" and 5½" boards

- Wood glue
- Paint
- Paintbrush
- Stencils
- Hot glue sticks
- Hot glue gun

- Hemp twine or jute

TOOLS

- Miter saw
- Palm sander

- Tape measure
- Scissors

TIME: 1 hour, plus dry time   **LEVEL:** Beginner

1. Cut various-sized squares and rectangles from the 3½" boards.

2. Using a miter saw, cut triangles from some of the 3½" boards and the 5½" boards. Vary the angles—I cut some with 15-degree, 20-degree, and 30-degree angles.

3. Cut 1" strips or pieces from some of the 5½" boards. You will need three pieces for each snowflake.

4. Lightly sand all the pieces.

5. Using wood glue, put two or three triangles together to make mountain ranges. Glue three of the 1" x 5½" pieces together to make snowflakes. Let the glue dry for a couple hours.

6. Paint the remaining rectangles and squares your desired color. I used red because it stands out so nicely on the green tree. Metallic colors look nice too. Be sure to paint both sides and the edges.

7. Using small image stencils of your choice, stencil images on the painted squares and rectangles. I used white paint for stenciling because it pops with the red.

8. When the glue is dry on the mountain ranges, use white paint and a small craft paintbrush to add "snow" to the top of the mountains.

9. Paint the snowflakes white. Be sure to paint both sides. Glitter paint would also look great on these.

10. You can hang the ornaments with wire threaded through small holes you drill. Or, my preferred method for ornament hangers is to use jute or hemp twine and hot glue. For the mountain ranges and rectangular pieces, cut 6" to 8" pieces of twine and knot two pieces together at the ends. For the snowflake ornaments, make some loop hangers with one piece of twine

11. Hot glue the twine hangers to the ornaments.

12. Use a hair dry set on low to blow away any hot glue strings.

PALLET POINTERS
MORE PALLET ORNAMENTS

The painted squares and rectangles can be used in lots of different ways. Decoupage favorite holiday memories, printed in black and white. Paint a monogram or initial or a favorite word on the square ornaments. Wrap the painted squares and rectangles in ribbon to make package ornaments. Other ornament ideas are to make trees or six-pointed stars from the triangle pieces. For the stars, be sure to cut the triangles at 30-degree angles. Make stick snowman from the 1" x 5½" pieces, tying bits of old wool sweaters around them for scarves. Use a small craft brush to paint face details and hot glue buttons on the snowmen.

DECORATIVE SKIS AND SLED

Winters in Montana mean plenty of snow, and snow means skiing, snowboarding, and sledding for my family. These decorative versions of a pair of skis and a sled are perfect décor items for the front porch or entryway, and they celebrate the winter season with simple designs that can be personalized to fit your style and home.

SUPPLIES

- Two 48" x 3½" x ¾" pallet boards
- Three 48" x 5½" x ¾" pallet boards
- Two notched 48" x 2" x 4" pallet runner boards

- Pencil
- 1" screws
- Two ¾" screws
- Two 2" screws
- 10" piece of a 1½" wide leather belt

- Paint
- Paintbrush
- Clear sealer
- Stain

TOOLS

- Jigsaw, band saw, or scroll saw
- Palm sander

- Drill
- Tape measure
- Straightedge

- Sharp scissors or X-Acto knife
- large plastic bowl or a paint can lid

TIME: 2 hours, plus dry time   **LEVEL:** Intermediate

FOR THE SKIS

1. Cut two 42" x 3½" x ¾" boards from the 48" x 3½" x ¾" pallet boards and set the scraps aside.

2. Draw a rounded ski tip on the end of one 42" board.

3. Use a jigsaw, band saw, or scroll saw to cut out the ski tip.

4. Trace the ski tip on the second 42" board and cut it out.

5. Sand the boards well, sanding the ski tip to have round edges and point.

6. From the ski tip, measure and mark the boards at 22" and at 28".

7. Draw a 6"-long rectangle with rounded corners between the areas marked off in the previous step.

8. Paint the rectangle black or another dark color.

9. Finish the skis as desired. I chose to stain the wood. If you are going to paint the skis, paint them *before* completing steps 6 through 8.

10. Cut the 10" leather belt piece in half lengthwise to make two 10" x ¾" pieces, using either sharp scissors or an X-Acto knife.

11. Place the leather strap or "binding" approximately 17" up from the bottom

of the ski and secure it with one ¾" screw screwed in through both ends of the leather strap and the ski. It should be centered over the painted rectangle. Predrill through the leather and the wood.

FOR THE SLED

1. Cut the two notched pallet runner boards to 30" long.

2. Cut one of the scrap notched pieces from step 1 to be 15" long, centering the notch.

3. From the bottom of the notch on the 30" board, draw a straight line as a cutting guide.

4. Draw a curved sled runner about 1⅝" away from the notch on the shorter side of the 30" board.

5. Using a jigsaw, band saw, or scroll saw, cut out the sled runner shape following the marks made in steps 3 and 4.

6. Repeat steps 3 through 5 with the second 30" notched board.

7. Cut three 22" x 5½" x ¾" boards and two 12" x 5½" x ¾" boards from the 48" x 5½" x ¾" pallet boards. Sand all of the boards.

8. Join the sled runner boards together with the 12" x 5½" x ¾" boards, placing one flat across the back ends of the runner boards and one about two thirds of the way up on the runner boards. Secure the 12" x 5½" x ¾" boards with two 1" screws per side.

9. Add the 15" notched 2" x 4" board to the top of the sled runner boards, placing

it about ½" away from the curved runners. Secure in place with two 2" screws, one on each side.

10. Lay the three 22" x 5½" x ¾" side by side. Using a large plastic bowl or a paint can lid, trace a curve on the top corners of the two outside boards.

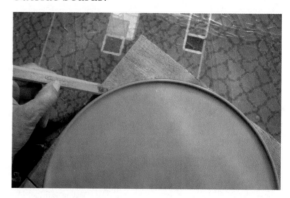

11. Cut the curves out with a jigsaw, band saw, or scroll saw.

12. Attach the three 22" x 5½" x ¾" boards to the sled runners, using two 1" screws per board, one screwed into each of the 12" boards added in step 8.

13. Paint as desired. I chose to paint the runners black and the sled seat blue. Because I wanted the sled "handle" unpainted and only stained, I removed it and stained it. I also could have taped off the areas I did not want painted or stained. I reattached the "handle" after everything was dry.

14. Decorate the sled as desired. I hand-lettered a favorite winter sentiment. You could stencil a saying, attach a winter wreath to the sled seat, or even attach a framed photo of your family sledding and enjoying the winter.

15. Finish with a clear sealer of choice.

RESOURCES

The stencils that were used on the porch pumpkin patch (page 70) can be purchased from Funky Junk's Old Sign Stencils at funkyjunkinteriors.com. Funky Junk's Old Sign Stencils offers several high-quality stencils that will look great on many of the pallet projects.

The letter stencils that were used on the garden tool stool (page 22), fishing pole holder (page 44), and firewood crate (page 74) and the woodland stencils that were used on the Christmas ornaments (page 116) are from Walmart.

The hooks that were used on the stocking hanger and shelf (page 108) and bottle opener that was used on the barbecue station (page 60) came from the Rustic Iron Store at rusticironstore.com. Rustic Iron Store sells a fantastic variety of handles and hooks at a low price.

You can find Fusion Mineral Paint at fusionmineralpaint.com. They have many beautiful colors, along with other products for painting and finishing wood and furniture.

I used a pallet buster to dismantle pallets. This tool is a great investment if you plan on building several pallet projects. Search for the Vestil Deluxe Pallet Buster on Amazon.com.

My favorite drills that I used for all projects are the Makita 18V cordless hammer and rotary drills. They are lightweight, yet powerful. Purchase at hardware stores such as Lowe's or Home Depot stores or online at makitatools.com.

My favorite jigsaw and sliding compound miter saws that I used for all projects are from DeWalt and can be purchased at www.dewalt.com or a local hardware store.

The stains that were used on projects are from MinWax. Find tips and colors at minwax.com.

Coconut oil was used as a finish on the harvest table and bench (page 89), and is Kirkland Signature brand from Costco.

Clear finishes used are Polycrylic by Minwax, Helmsman Spar Urethane by Minwax, and Rust-Oleum's American Accents Ultra Cover X2. Each of these can be found at most hardware stores or Walmart.

ACKNOWLEDGMENTS

As with anything worthwhile in life, this book would not have happened without the help, encouragement, and support of others. To my family, Paul, Tate, Keldon, and Tessa: Thank you for putting up with my crazy ideas, for being there for me, and for pushing me out of my comfort zone. You are the reason I work harder and strive to be better each day.

To my friends, especially Missy and Rachel, who checked in with me often to see how the book was coming along and who encouraged me in the process: Thank you. To my blogging friends and readers, your comments and questions inspire me to continue to create, innovate, and share new things.

ABOUT THE AUTHOR

Becky Lamb is a builder, junker, repurposer, blogger, crafter, retired teacher, wife, and mother of three. Her work has been featured in *Country Home, GreenCraft Magazine,* and on the television show *Home and Family*. Becky has been crafting and creating as long as she can remember. She discovered her love for building in 2000, when she started to sell home décor items at local shows and markets. In 2008, she started writing about and sharing her building and creating adventures on her blog, *Beyond the Picket Fence*. When not building, Becky enjoys working on projects in her home, a 1931 schoolhouse, and spending time outdoors with her family in her home state of Montana.

Tessa Lamb